THIS
or
THAT?
2
or

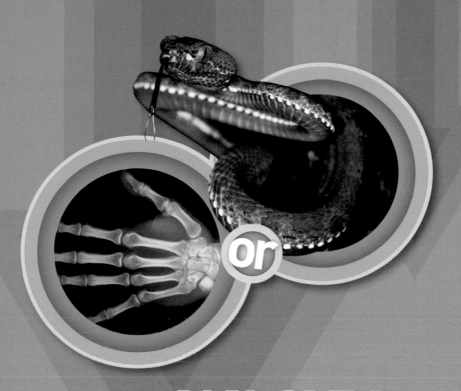

MORE **WACKY** CHOICES

TO REVEAL THE
HIDDEN
YOU

JR MORTIMER

NATIONAL GEOGRAPHIC KiDS

WASHINGTON, D.C.

The National Geographic Society is one of the world's largest nonprofit scientific and educational organizations. Founded in 1888 to "increase and diffuse geographic knowledge," the member-supported Society works to inspire people to care about the planet. Through its online community, members can get closer to explorers and photographers, connect with other members around the world and help make a difference. National Geographic reflects the world through its magazines, television programs, films, books, DVDs, radio, maps, exhibitions, live events, school publishing programs, interactive media and merchandise. National Geographic magazine, the Society's official journal, published in English and 39 local-language editions, is read by more than 60 million people each month. The National Geographic Channel reaches 440 million households in 171 countries in 48 languages. National Geographic Digital Media receives more than 27 million visitors a month. National Geographic has funded more than 10,000 scientific research, conservation and exploration projects and supports an education program promoting geographic literacy.

For more information, please visit www.nationalgeographic.com, call 1-800-NGS LINE (647-5463), or write to the following address:
National Geographic Society
1145 17th Street N.W.
Washington, D.C. 20036-4688 U.S.A.

Visit us online at nationalgeographic.com/books

For librarians and teachers: ngchildrensbooks.org

More for kids from National Geographic: kids.nationalgeographic.com

For information about special discounts for bulk purchases, please contact National Geographic Books Special Sales: ngspecsales@ngs.org

For rights or permissions inquiries, please contact National Geographic Books Subsidiary Rights: ngbookrights@ngs.org

Paperback ISBN: 978-1-4263-1719-4
Reinforced library edition ISBN: 978-1-4263-1720-0

Printed in the United States of America
14/QGT-CML/1

TABLE OF CONTENTS

GET PICKY!

CHOOSE THIS:
Wear a comfortable shirt to school.

CHOOSE THAT:
Dress up and impress your friends.

CHOOSE THIS:
Bring your lunch from home.

CHOOSE THAT:
Eat what they're serving in the cafeteria.

CHOOSE THIS:
Buy the newest video game.

CHOOSE THAT:
Save up and get a new system later.

DECISIONS! DECISIONS!

Every minute of every day we make choices about how we spend our time, what we like, and how we interact with one another. Most are minor, but when you add them all up, your decisions reveal what makes you *you!* THIS or THAT? WHICH WILL IT BE?

WELCOME TO THE BOOK OF CHOICES. Want to find out what superpowers would suit you? Or how about your dream career? Each chapter offers you a series of options—some silly, some serious, some downright spectacular, and some a little gross. Don't worry about making a wrong choice—there are none. The whole point is to enjoy yourself. If you've ever been called picky, get ready for loads of fun! In *This or That? 2,* it's a GOOD thing!

DECISIONS, DECISIONS

KEEP COUNT
OF EACH TIME YOU CHOOSE

THIS!
or THAT!

AT THE END OF EACH CHAPTER OF *THIS OR THAT? 2*, you'll get some professional help from **Dr. Matt Bellace.** He's a **psychologist** and **stand-up comedian.** Dr. Bellace will analyze your choices and determine what your decisions say about you. Through exploration and analysis of the inner workings of your mind, he'll peel you back layer by layer and **you won't even realize it!** But keep in mind these scenarios are just for fun. Don't like your results?

TAKE THE QUIZ AGAIN!

CHAPTER 1

MUTANT POWERS

Wouldn't it be great to have special powers like the characters from X-Men? Or the gods and goddesses of Greek mythology? Each page in this chapter offers a choice between awesome talents that would give you an edge over your friends and enemies. But be warned! Use these abilities for good—not evil—or you'll find yourself super-grounded.

CHOOSE
THIS:

You have **living snakes** for your hair, like **Medusa.**

statue of Medusa

or

CHOOSE
THAT:

You have **multiple heads,** like Hydra.

MUSE BEFORE YOU CHOOSE

*Sss*super-cool hairdo. Combing is tricky. More heads are better than one. More mouths to feed.

If you CHOSE THIS: ⬇

You won't fight your battles alone if your locks are like Medusa's. With hair made of **POISONOUS SNAKES** like the **NOSE-HORNED VIPER,** you can rest assured that you'll have the upper hand over enemies. This viper is one of the most common types of poisonous snake in Europe, and its venom leaves victims destined for **DEATH** unless treated right away. These are some *sssuper*-lethal sidekicks!

nose-horned viper

If you CHOSE ⬇THAT:

If you're like Hydra, you're extremely difficult to kill. In Greek mythology, Hydra was a serpent-like monster with **MANY HEADS.** If you cut off one head, two more would grow in its place, making it nearly impossible to defeat. That's the situation with the pesky **NOMURA'S JELLYFISH,** found mostly in the

Nomura's jellyfish

waters near China and Japan. Due to possible overfishing and rising water temperatures, this tentacular villain swarms in alarmingly huge numbers, disrupting water-treatment plants and destroying oceanic wildlife. These jellyfish are nearly impossible to defeat, because when they are threatened they release billions of sperm or eggs that attach to rocks and later grow into **MORE JELLYFISH.** Asian governments are forming alliances to stop this modern-day Hydra.

Hercules defeating Hydra

11

CHOOSE THIS:

Your **tail** delivers a **stunning slap.**

or

CHOOSE THAT:

Your **tongue** delivers a powerful **punch.**

MUSE BEFORE YOU CHOOSE

Immobilized prey. Hard to see what you're slapping.
Entertaining boxing match. Unwanted drool.

If you CHOSE ⬇THIS:

Don't be embarrassed by your stunning rear end if you're like the thresher shark. This shark has a tail so large that it accounts for a **THIRD OF ITS BODY WEIGHT,** and it uses it like a bullwhip to slap prey. Thresher sharks swim at high speeds in short bursts, unleashing quick slaps of their tails and leaving fish **STUNNED** by the impact. As the fish gather their senses, the sharks devour them in a yummy gulp. That's one talented tail!

thresher shark

If you CHOSE THAT:⬇

A powerful tongue can come in handy. Consider the giant palm salamander *(Bolitoglossa dofleini)* of Central America, which is known to have the **STRONGEST MUSCLE** in the animal world. The elastic fibers in its mouth stretch to store up energy and then release its tongue with more than **18,000 WATTS** of power per kilogram of muscle. That's quite a punch! Bugs don't see it coming—the sticky tip snags its prey in just a few thousandths of a second, about **50 TIMES FASTER** than the blink of an eye. This ability could come in handy at the dinner table!

giant palm salamander

Think Twice!

Another animal with a powerful punch is the gorilla. If you were in a boxing match with one of these guys, you'd most likely lose. A gorilla's upper body strength is about six times stronger than a human's.

13

CHOOSE THIS:

You can bring extinct animals back to life.

or

CHOOSE THAT:

You have the ability to talk with animals.

MUSE BEFORE YOU CHOOSE

Pet dinosaurs! You might get eaten. Juicy animal gossip. Quiet moments are rare.

Tyrannosaurus rex

If you CHOSE THIS:

Scientists estimate that 99.9 percent of all the life-forms that have ever lived on Earth are now **EXTINCT**. But what if you could bring some of them back? Advances in biotechnology are allowing humans to experiment with **RESURRECTING** long-gone species, but should we? Just bringing animals back to life doesn't mean they can survive in today's world. After all, Earth doesn't look the same as it did when **WOOLLY MAMMOTHS** roamed the planet!

If you CHOSE THAT:

You want to be **DR. DOOLITTLE**, eh? Two steps ahead of you is Professor Con Slobodchikoff from Northern Arizona University. His research has nearly broken the language barrier between humans and animals—especially **PRAIRIE DOGS**. For more than 30 years, the professor has deciphered animal communications by recording the sounds animals make and analyzing the context in which the sounds are made. Prairie dogs will make a specific sound for a **PREDATOR** like a coyote that is different from the sound they make for a dog. They can even tell their friends what color shirt a human is wearing!

Choice Nugget

Unlocking the secrets of animal communication is kind of like translating an ancient, forgotten language. Scientists look for keys that will reveal patterns, much like the Rosetta stone did for Egyptian hieroglyphics.

prairie dogs

15

CHOOSE THIS:

You have **acid spit,** but you frequently **pee** on yourself.

vultures

or

CHOOSE THAT:

You can turn things into **stone,** but your **friends** think you're **creepy.**

gargoyle statue in Paris, France

MUSE BEFORE YOU CHOOSE

The WORST bad breath. Diapers ... again. No holding hands with your sweetheart. Social outcast.

If you CHOSE ⬇THIS:

If you can spit acid, think of the tooth-brushes you'll (literally) **BURN THROUGH!** You won't be alone with your deadly digestive juices, however. The vulture also has one of the most **CONCENTRATED STOMACH ACIDS** in the animal kingdom. Because vultures feast on dead animals, the birds' bellies are able to kill most diseases and can even dissolve metal (if it ever finds its way in there). The birds are also famous for peeing on themselves to **DISINFECT** their feathers and feet from the harmful bacteria picked up while tearing into their meals. With this superpower, it's safe to say your life will be FULL of awkward moments!

If you CHOSE ⬇THAT:

If gargoyles get you excited, take a lesson from one of the **CREEPIEST PLACES** in the world, Lake Natron in Tanzania, where animals look like they've been turned into **STONE** if submerged in the water. Resembling the scene of a horror movie, this ghostly (and rare) phenomenon is caused by the high levels of sodium carbonate and salt, from **VOLCANIC ASH**, in the lake. If confused birds or bats fly into its mirrored surface, they're not likely to come out, because their bodies will dry and harden into statues. In his book *Across the Ravaged Land,* photographer Nick Brandt arranged these **PETRIFIED ANIMALS** into haunting scenes.

Think Twice!

Natron—the mineral salt for which Lake Natron is named— was used by the ancient Egyptians in their mummification rituals.

CHOOSE THIS:

You can see far into the future.

or

CHOOSE THAT:

You can see way, way back into the past.

MUSE
BEFORE YOU CHOOSE

You'll know the winning lottery numbers. You'll never be surprised. You can tell us how the pyramids were built. No need for history books.

If you CHOSE THIS:

You don't have to be psychic to see far into the **FUTURE.** Earth's scientists do it every day. The men and women conducting research in **PHYSICS, MATHEMATICS, GEOLOGY, AND PLANETARY SCIENCE** are building our knowledge of the natural world so we can look ahead to what's around the corner. They ask questions like, When will Earth undergo another ice age? And how long will **PHOBOS**—one of Mars's moons—continue to orbit the red planet before it gets too close and explodes? That makes scientists kind of like our modern-day fortune-tellers!

If you CHOSE THAT:

If you've got the ability to see into the past, then there's no need for you to stop by a **TIME CAPSULE** in Seward, Nebraska, U.S.A.! The **45-TON** (40,823 kg) vault was buried and sealed in 1975 by Harold Keith Davisson, a local store owner and town character. Inside is a varied assortment of **5,000 ITEMS** from the disco era, including a car. It will be opened on **JULY 4, 2025,** but with your superpower, its contents will probably tell you what you already know!

Choice Nugget

In 2006, the Internet company Yahoo! gathered the first digital time capsule, with 170,857 pictures, videos, songs, and stories submitted by people from all over the world.

19

CHOOSE THIS:

You can **control** the **wind,** like the **Anemoi.**

or

CHOOSE THAT:

You can **control** the **seas,** like **Poseidon.**

Poseidon

MUSE BEFORE YOU CHOOSE

The breeze is perfect for a hot air balloon ride or flying a kite. The waves are always good for surfing.

If you CHOSE ⬇THIS:

Just like the **ANEMOI**, the wind gods from Greek mythology, having control over the breeze is great power. Even though people harnessed the wind with **SAILBOATS AND WINDMILLS** hundreds of years ago, it wasn't until the past decade that large, 200-foot (60.96 m) wind turbines became a popular energy source. Turbines catch the wind with their propeller-like blades and then convert the **KINETIC ENERGY** (the motion) into electric current. Wind is a clean renewable resource that produces no air or water pollution, and since it's **FREE,** the costs are nearly zero once the turbine is built. So having power over the wind isn't just good for the environment, it's good for your wallet, too.

▲ Anemoi

If you CHOSE ⬇THAT:

If you have abilities like **POSEIDON**—the mythological Greek god who ruled the seas—be sure to make use of the forces of falling water. In what's known as **HYDROPOWER,** moving water pushes its way through machines called **TURBINES,** which generate electricity humans can use. A good example is found in Washington State, U.S.A., at the **GRAND COULEE DAM**—the largest hydropower generator in the United States. It's almost a mile (1.6 km) long!

Choice Nugget

The world's oldest windmills are located in Iran and Afghanistan and were used to grind grain.

THIS:
X-ray
vision

or

CHOOSE

THAT:
Night vision

MUSE BEFORE YOU CHOOSE

See through buildings. Know for sure when you've broken a bone. The basement won't seem so scary. You're in charge if there's a blackout.

22

If you CHOSE ⬇THIS:

Before you get excited about x-ray vision, you should consider something new: **T-RAY VISION**. Terahertz rays (t-rays) are not as harmful as x-rays, but they can achieve the same effect of seeing through things. The reason you may not have heard of them is because t-ray scanning equipment has been large and expensive, so nobody really used it. But recently researchers have overcome that problem by making a terahertz chip about the **SIZE OF A PENNY** that could fit into a smartphone. That means in the near future you could hold up a phone and know if somebody has broken a bone!

If you CHOSE THAT: ⬇

You'll **NEVER FUMBLE AROUND IN THE DARK AGAIN!** Thermal imaging with infrared light is a type of night vision that detects differences in the temperature between background and foreground objects. You'll be in an exclusive club if your eyes have the "sixth sense" of **DETECTING INFRA-RED LIGHT**—vampire bats and some species of snake, including the mangrove viper, are known to do this. The **PIT ORGAN** in their unique sensory system allows them to know how far away they are from a target.

mangrove viper

CHOOSE **THIS:**

Your **fingers freeze** water.

or

CHOOSE **THAT:**

Your **toes** help you **walk** on **water.**

MUSE
BEFORE YOU
CHOOSE

Beverages are always cold. Chilly showers. No surfboard required. Trip on waves.

24

If you CHOSE ⬇THIS:

Subarctic digits sound appealing, eh? Then check out the bizarre phenomenon known as the **BRINICLE**, an **ICY "FINGER"** that moves through Arctic and Antarctic waters, **FREEZING EVERYTHING IN ITS PATH.** This icicle of death occurs when warmer seawater collides with the ice sheet above and new ice is formed. Salt is concentrated into a liquid called brine, and because it is denser and much colder than the surrounding seawater, a web of ice slowly sinks, freezing everything it touches, including sea urchins and sea stars. So, be sure to remember, with this power it is **ESPECIALLY RUDE** to point your finger at someone!

diver filming brinicles in McMurdo Sound, Antarctica

If you CHOSE THAT:⬇

If you're a jacana, you can't *actually* walk on water, but it sure looks like it. This bird has **EXTRA-LONG TOENAILS** that spread its body weight over large areas, allowing it to run across aquatic plants as if **DEFYING GRAVITY.** Jacanas love to feast on the snails, bugs, and fish hanging out among floating plants, and their feet evolved to become quite useful for walking in those hard-to-reach places. With this **SUPERPOWER,** not only will you enjoy impressing your friends at the swimming pool, you'll also be able to get a snail snack if you get hungry!

jacana

ANALYZE THIS!

If you mostly picked **CHOOSE THIS,** you love making bold moves and standing out from the crowd. Your personality is one of a kind, and you really thrive in the spotlight. Just remember that being the center of attention can come with a price—your dominant attitude definitely grabs people's attention, but some of that is bound to be negative. It's okay to be the star, but make sure your friends don't feel shoved aside. If you really want to be adored, make sure to share the spotlight. A kind and thoughtful personality will take you from star to superstar!

ANALYZE THAT!

If you mostly picked **CHOOSE THAT,** you're the quiet type with a mysterious side. You may seem as placid as the surface of a lake, but who knows what deep currents run beneath your calm exterior. Your personality may be straightforward and ordered, but you're drawn to the unseen and the unknown. Others may not understand your complex nature at first glance, but don't worry—once people get to know you, they will appreciate your unique viewpoints and ways of living.

CHAPTER 2

EXTREME ADVENTURE

We humans love exploring the great unknowns and pushing ourselves to the extreme. Are you ready for your big adventure? This chapter will prepare you for some situations that could mean life or death—and some that are just cool to think about. Live life on the edge and never look back!

THIS:

Drive **through** the **eye** of a **tornado.**

or

THAT:

Climb an **erupting** volcano.

MUSE BEFORE YOU CHOOSE High-speed winds. Flying debris. Unexpected explosions. HOT HOT HOT.

If you CHOSE THIS: →

You don't want to find yourself near the path of a **TORNADO** unless, well, it's your job! **STORM CHASERS** built The Dominator 2 to withstand high winds and flying debris, allowing scientists to study the storms up close. Weighing 8,000 pounds (3,629 kg), this SUV has two layers of special protective glass and an outer shell of thick steel. Three sets of superstrong windshield wipers are required to keep a clear view for the driver. But just because this **ARMORED CAR** is equipped to hold up in a tornado, don't think storm chasers sit back for a nice cruise. They still hang on for the ride of a lifetime!

a massive category F4 tornado

If you CHOSE ↓THAT:

Things are going to heat up if you follow in the footsteps of **GEOFF MACKLEY,** who descended 500 yards (457 m) into the pit of an active volcano near Australia. Equipped with only a silver **PROTECTIVE SUIT** and oxygen canisters, Mackley was able to get within 100 yards (91 m) of the **BOILING LAVA** before running out of rope. Even though it is believed he is the only human to have ever gotten that close to a volcano's core, Mackley says he would have gone farther if he'd had enough rope.

eruption of Mount Yasur on Tanna Island, Vanuatu

CHOOSE **THIS:**

Lie in a **bed** with **scorpions.**

or

CHOOSE **THAT:**

Get **stuck** in a swarm of **killer bees.**

MUSE BEFORE YOU CHOOSE

Either way you're getting stung ... poor you!

scorpion

If you CHOSE ⬇ THIS:

You'll be happy to hear that most **SCORPION STINGS**—while painful— are mostly harmless. There are as many as 1,500 **SCORPION SPECIES** worldwide, yet only about 30 have potentially fatal stings. But if you happen to be stung, you should still seek medical treatment just to be sure you haven't found yourself injected with **POISONOUS TOXINS.**

If you CHOSE THAT: ⬇

Bzzzzzzz! When you hear the buzz of **KILLER BEES**, don't start swatting like a maniac— that will only anger them more. You've come into their territory, and a **HIVE** must be nearby. Cover your face and neck with your shirt and do your best to **RETREAT CALMLY** without sudden movements or loud noises. If they're still after you, pick up the pace and get outta there! They'll quit once you're far enough away from the hive, usually about 200 yards (183 m).

killer bees

Think Twice!

Diving into water won't save you from killer bees. They will hover and attack when you come up for air.

CHOOSE

THIS:

Go **2 months** without **food.**

or

CHOOSE

THAT:

Go **5 days** without **water.**

MUSE BEFORE YOU CHOOSE

You won't have to worry about cooking. Stomach pangs. No pee breaks! Cotton mouth.

If you CHOSE THIS: ↓

You'll be fantasizing about ICE-CREAM SUNDAES if you have to go without eating for a long stretch, but it PROBABLY WON'T KILL YOU. Most doctors agree that humans can go about eight weeks without food and survive, AS LONG AS WE HAVE WATER. People have gone longer and were okay, and some have starved in less time—the length of time mainly has to do with how physically fit you are, how much fat you have on your body that can be burned up, and even how determined you are. You're also more likely to survive longer without food if you're in a temperate climate—one that's not too cold or too hot.

If you CHOSE ↓THAT:

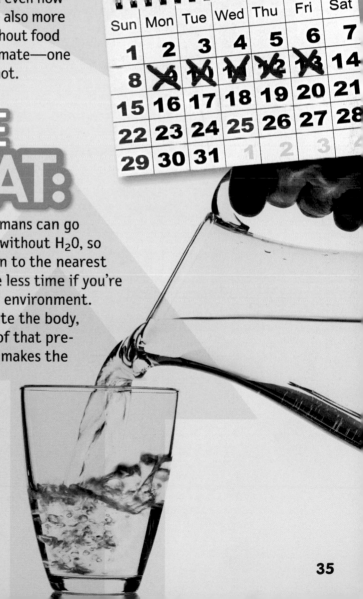

You could die of thirst! Humans can go only THREE TO FIVE DAYS without H_2O, so put this book down and run to the nearest water fountain. You'll have less time if you're in a superhot or supercold environment. Extreme heat will dehydrate the body, and you'll sweat out a lot of that precious water. Extreme cold makes the body WORK EXTRA HARD to keep that 98.6°F (37°C) it likes so much, which eats into your internal water supply.

35

CHOOSE THIS:

Spend 2 weeks in the world's deepest cave.

or

CHOOSE THAT:

MUSE BEFORE YOU CHOOSE

Constant temperature. That's half a month! Sharks are sometimes around other pretty fishes. Supersharp pearly whites.

Scuba dive in shark-infested waters for 1 hour.

If you CHOSE THIS:

Two weeks is a long time to spend in **KRUBERA**—the world's deepest known cave, located in the country of Georgia—but some expeditions have lasted as long as a month. You'll pass through an intricate number of **CRAMPED PASSAGES**, massive caverns, huge pits, and ice-cold water, so be ready for some intense exploring. The deepest known spot in Krubera is at 6,824 feet (2,080 m)—**MORE THAN A MILE (1.6 KM) BELOW** Earth's surface!

Choice Nugget

Surfers account for about 50% of shark attacks in the United States.

If you CHOSE THAT:

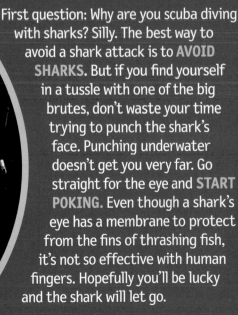

First question: Why are you scuba diving with sharks? Silly. The best way to avoid a shark attack is to **AVOID SHARKS.** But if you find yourself in a tussle with one of the big brutes, don't waste your time trying to punch the shark's face. Punching underwater doesn't get you very far. Go straight for the eye and **START POKING.** Even though a shark's eye has a membrane to protect from the fins of thrashing fish, it's not so effective with human fingers. Hopefully you'll be lucky and the shark will let go.

CHOOSE **THIS:**

Wet and **hot**

or

CHOOSE **THAT:**

Dry and **Cold**

MUSE
BEFORE YOU
CHOOSE

Monsoon season. Sweating through your clothes. Long underwear. Chapped lips.

If you CHOSE ⬇THIS:

Don't waste your time sing-
ing "Rain, rain, go away. Come
again another day." The AGUMBE
RAINFOREST RESEARCH STATION
(ARRS) is in one of the wettest places
in India, so you'll just have to get used
to water being a part of everything you
do. This small research facility is located in
the state of KARNATAKA where it rains up to 280
inches (711 cm) every year. Scientists and volunteers come
here to study the wildlife, especially KING COBRAS, the longest venomous snakes
in the world. These passionate researchers overlook the extreme heat and rain
for the chance to live alongside the animals in the heart of the rain forest.

If you CHOSE THAT:⬇

Cool off a while and spend your winter at the SOUTH POLE OBSERVATORY
(SPO) in Antarctica. The National Oceanic and Atmospheric Administra-
tion (NOAA) continually monitors gases and particles in the atmosphere
year-round, even through the six-month
winter of darkness. Yes, you read that
correctly ... SIX MONTHS OF NO
SUN. But don't think it's all bad
in this extreme environment,
where temperatures can
reach minus 140°F (–95°C).
The scientists who "winter
over" at the South Pole
say it's the best spot on
the planet to SEE THE
STARS. Without any light
from buildings or sky-
scrapers, you can see
them all day long.

gentoo penguins

39

CHOOSE

THIS:
No strings attached

or

CHOOSE

THAT:
Dangle from a wire

MUSE BEFORE YOU CHOOSE

Fly like a bird. No safety net! Feel more secure. No freedom to explore.

40

If you CHOSE ⬇THIS:

Let the wind whip you left, then right, as you soar above the **ALPS** in your **HANG GLIDER**. Interlaken, Switzerland, is rated one of the best places in the world for hang gliding, due to its relatively mild weather conditions and beautiful sights. Many gliders are equipped with an **ONBOARD COMPUTER**, gadgets that detect wind speed, air pressure, and altitude, and reserve **PARACHUTES** in case of emergency. Get ready to spread your wings and **FLY**!

Think Twice!

Leonardo da Vinci sketched drawings of early hang gliders in the 1400s.

If you CHOSE ⬇THAT:

If the safety of a wire sounds more appealing to you, strap on a harness and get ready to zip-line! Check out Icy Strait Point in Alaska, U.S.A., home to the **ZIPRIDER**—which claims to be the world's longest zip line. The **MILE-LONG** (1.6 km) ride first takes you down a 1,320-foot (402 m) vertical drop before hitting top speeds of **65 MILES AN HOUR** (105 kph). This adrenaline-pumping rush will last only 90 seconds, and you'll want to do it again!

CHOOSE THIS:

Lost in the woods

or

CHOOSE THAT:

MUSE BEFORE YOU CHOOSE

Grizzly bears. Poisonous berries. Hurricanes. Seasickness.

Adrift at sea

If you CHOSE THIS:

Does that tree look like one you passed an hour ago? Have you stepped on this rock before? Both are valid questions, but hey ... you might be ... um ... **LOST.** Take a deep breath and stay in control. Hopefully you told someone you were going into the woods for a **HIKE.** They will notice (eventually) that you haven't returned and will form a search crew. In the meantime, find a dry, flat place to hang out, ideally near a **WATER** source, and **STAY PUT.** But don't be tempted to dip your canteen in that river or stream unless you get desperate—most bodies of fresh water are contaminated with microorganisms, so you may be better off collecting **RAINWATER** or the **DEW** off plants instead. When you hear search crews, scream like you're at a pep rally!

If you CHOSE THAT:

Ahoy! What a predicament you've gotten yourself into! Being **STRANDED AT SEA** is a sticky situation, so having your wits about you is key. **TIE EVERYTHING DOWN**— you wouldn't want a big wave to toss your last snack out of the boat. Whatever you do, DON'T drink seawater—it will dry you out. And while you're at it, make friends with any birds you see flying around. Many **SEA-BIRDS** hunt during the day and return to land at dusk, so follow them to land ho!

ANALYZE
THIS!

If you mostly picked **CHOOSE THIS,** then you may be wise beyond your years—you like to mix your extreme adventures with a good dose of caution. You're open to trying new things and having adventures as long as they're reasonably safe. After all, there's no point in taking a trip that you won't survive to brag about! Others likely rely on you for advice and admire your good sense. However, it's important to remember that some of the best experiences can come from stepping outside your comfort zone.

ANALYZE
THAT!

If you mostly picked **CHOOSE THAT,** then you have the makings of a true daredevil! A certified thrill seeker, you live life on the edge and enjoy testing your limits. Your adventurous attitude will lead you to lots of new foods, places, and experiences, and you'll never encounter a dull moment. Just remember that safety is a virtue, too. After all, you'll want to stay safe so you can get to the next adventure!

CHAPTER ③

ALL ABOARD!

Does your hometown sometimes make you so bored you want to hit your head against the wall? Well, there's no need for a concussion. Just pack your bags and get going. This chapter is all about the destinations you never knew you wanted to visit. Who knows? You might never come back!

CHOOSE THIS:

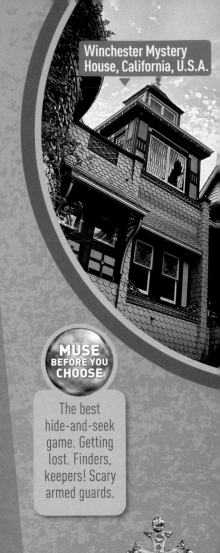

Winchester Mystery House, California, U.S.A.

Sneak around some secret passageways.

or

CHOOSE THAT:

MUSE BEFORE YOU CHOOSE

The best hide-and-seek game. Getting lost. Finders, keepers! Scary armed guards.

St. Edward's Crown

Sneak a peek at priceless jewels.

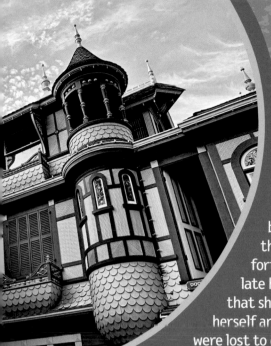

IF YOU CHOSE THIS:

Don't get lost as you creep through the passages at the **WINCHESTER MYSTERY HOUSE** in San Jose, California, U.S.A. Construction on the house began in 1884, when Sarah Winchester—the heiress to the Winchester rifle fortune—was mourning the loss of her late husband. She was told by a **PSYCHIC** that she must continuously build a home for herself and the **GHOSTS** of all people whose lives were lost to gunshot wounds. Until Sarah's death 38 years later, a construction crew remained on-site tirelessly building. This resulted in odd effects like stairs that lead to the ceiling and doors that open into walls!

IF YOU CHOSE THAT:

You won't actually have to sneak a peek at the **CROWN JEWELS** in the Tower of London in England, but chances are you'll have to wait in line. Every year millions of visitors flock to this gallery of bling worn by kings and queens for hundreds of years. Here you'll find the First Star of Africa—the largest flawless cut diamond in the world—mounted atop the Sovereign's Sceptre, a gold rod that is used in royal ceremonies. But gold and jewels aren't the only things you'll find—the **TOWER OF LONDON** was the country's most famous prison, and you can also tour the arsenal of weapons and medieval **TORTURE CHAMBERS**. Don't stick around after closing hours though—some say the tower is haunted!

Choice Nugget

According to a popular suspicion in the 1800s, ghosts hated mirrors because their reflection caused them to vanish.

If you CHOSE THIS: ⬇

You'll *literally* chill out if your new buddy is the Abominable Snowman, also known as the YETI. Legend has it the mysterious creature roams the Himalaya mountains of TIBET, where temperatures can reach minus 31°F (–35°C) up on Mount Everest. But don't break out your sleeping bag just yet. New research suggests that the Yeti may actually be a long-lost relative of the POLAR BEAR, not the terrifying creature of MYTH. Either way, you might want to look for a new snuggle buddy.

If you CHOSE THAT: ⬇

You'll push your body to the extreme if you get wet with "NESSIE," the legendary beast said to swim the vast waters of LOCH NESS, a lake in the Highlands of Scotland known for being very cold and very deep—up to 700 feet (213 m). Swimming here is usually reserved for experienced open-water athletes, so you'll need some vigorous training before meeting the MONSTER that supposedly lurks beneath the surface. Nessie may prove to be a bit shy, so you might have to settle for land-based activities, like visiting the ruins of nearby URQUHART CASTLE. Built some 800 years ago, the castle is one of the most visited sites in all of SCOTLAND.

CHOOSE **THIS:**

Rest and **relaxation**

or

CHOOSE **THAT:**

Thrills and **chills**

MUSE
BEFORE YOU
CHOOSE

Relieve some stress. Who has time for R&R? Live on the edge. Anxiety.

If you CHOSE THIS: ⬇

Take it easy as your boat cruises along the vast **NETWORK OF CANALS** of Amsterdam in the Netherlands. Constructed mostly in the 1600s, the **WATERWAYS** are arranged into three concentric semicircles around the city center, with many smaller canals fanning out. Besides being beautiful, the canals are a great way to get around the city. But if you're looking for a little peace and quiet, be sure not to book your trip on one of the national holidays. The canals become a **PARADE ROUTE**, and thousands of people come out to party!

canal in Amsterdam, Netherlands

If you CHOSE THAT: ⬇

Buckle up, because you're on the **KINGDA KA**, the tallest **ROLLER COASTER** in the world and the fastest in North America. You'll zoom from 0 to **128 MILES AN HOUR** (206 kph) in three and a half seconds and shoot 456 feet (139 m) into the sky. That's about the height of a **45-STORY BUILDING.** You can find this ride at Six Flags Great Adventure in Jackson, New Jersey, U.S.A.

Kingda Ka roller coaster, New Jersey, U.S.A.

Choice Nugget

The first roller coaster in the U.S.A. opened in Coney Island, New York, in 1884 and cost a nickel to ride.

CHOOSE THIS:

Sleep in a building made of ice.

or

CHOOSE THAT:

MUSE BEFORE YOU CHOOSE

Brrrrrrr! Chilly dreams. Finding the front door—and the toilet!

Use the bathroom in an invisible building.

If you CHOSE THIS:

Stay at the **HÔTEL DE GLACE**, the ice hotel on the outskirts of Quebec City, Canada, which has beds made of **ICE** and maintains a temperature of about **26°F** (–3°C). Built every December for a grand opening in January, the Hôtel de Glace takes 50 people more than a month and a half, 500 tons (450 mT) of ice, and 30,000 tons (27,215 mT) of **SNOW** to construct. A night or two in this frosty destination will certainly be a vacation to remember!

Hôtel de Glace

If you CHOSE THAT:

Now you see it, now you don't! That's what you'll say when you visit the **TOWER INFINITY** in Seoul, South Korea, the world's first "**INVISIBLE**" **SKYSCRAPER**. But don't pack your bags just yet—the 1,476-feet-tall (450 m) building is still in design, and the architects have not given a date they expect it to be finished. The invisibility effect will be achieved by a series of cameras placed at different heights that take in the **SURROUNDING VIEW** and then **PROJECT THE IMAGES** onto rows of LED screens on the building's exterior. Tower Infinity's transparency can be turned on and off by increasing the intensity of the LED screens. And don't worry about finding the bathroom—only the *outside* of the building will be invisible!

Choice Nugget

A seven-story office building in Newark, Ohio, U.S.A., was built to look like a giant picnic basket.

THIS:

Ride a **hot air balloon**, but in **crowded** skies.

or

CHOOSE

THAT:

camel

Ride a **stinky camel**, but in open **space**.

MUSE BEFORE YOU CHOOSE

Spectacular views. Air collisions.
Room to roam. Serious body odor.

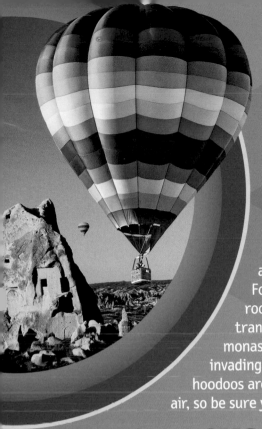

If you CHOSE ⬇THIS:

You won't soar the skies alone in **CAPPADOCIA**, Turkey, a popular destination for balloon enthusiasts. The region is famous for its "**FAIRY CHIMNEYS**"—tall, thin rock formations called hoodoos that were carved out and made into buildings by early settlers. Formed from the erosion of sedimentary rocks, the magnificent structures were transformed into houses, churches, and monasteries, and served as protection from invading armies for **THOUSANDS OF YEARS**. The hoodoos are a unique attraction to see from the air, so be sure you steer clear of your balloon buddies!

If you CHOSE ⬇THAT:

You might pinch your nose while camel trekking in the Northern Territory of **AUSTRALIA**, but at least you'll have plenty of room to explore. The barren region is home to a sandstone landmark called **AYERS ROCK** that juts 1,142 feet (348 m) into the air. Guided camel tours will take you to the 400-million-year-old rock, but you'll have to excuse your ride's potent odor. Camels' smell is a combination of their urine, feces, and spit, which is a regurgitation of **STOMACH JUICES**. Some say you can smell a camel before you see it!

Choice Nugget

Check out the hoodoos in Bryce Canyon National Park in Utah, U.S.A. They were formed primarily by a geological process called frost wedging, which happens when water from melting snow seeps into cracks in the rocks and freezes at night. Because water expands when it freezes, this wedging pries open the cracks.

CHOOSE
THIS:
Zoom **down** a **slippery** slope.

or

CHOOSE
THAT:
Skate **around** a **giant** pipe.

MUSE BEFORE YOU CHOOSE Feel the need for speed. Wipeouts. Awesome flips. Scrapes and bruises.

If you CHOSE ⬇ THIS:

If hurtling down a mountainside is your thing, you might want to check out **VAIL**, Colorado, U.S.A. This resort town is located at the base of Vail Mountain, which is widely regarded as one of the **BEST SNOW-BOARDING DESTINATIONS** in America. With 5,289 acres (2,140 ha) of available terrain, you're likely to find fresh snow that hasn't been ridden on by anyone else. But that's not the only reason Vail is so popular—the town's roads are heated, so snowboarders don't even have to set foot in the snow to get to the lifts!

If you CHOSE ⬇ THAT:

Grab your board and head to Louisville Extreme Park in Louisville, Kentucky, U.S.A., which features more than **40,000 SQUARE FEET** (3,716 sq m) of outdoor concrete skating surface. Start out with an **OLLIE**—a jump performed by tapping the tail of the board on the ground—and work your way up to a **McTWIST**, where you fly off a ramp and turn 540 degrees. For the more experienced skaters, the park has a 24-foot (7 m) full-pipe and a wooden vert ramp—but don't worry if none of that makes sense to you. The park welcomes people of all ages and skill levels. Just be sure to wear your protective gear!

Choice Nugget

The first Olympic snowboarding event was at the 1998 Winter Games in Nagano, Japan.

CHOOSE THIS:

Get **your** groove on with a **blue**-footed **booby.**

or

CHOOSE THAT:

Play **hopscotch** with a **tomato** frog.

MUSE BEFORE YOU CHOOSE   Show off your mad skills. You might get pecked. Jumping contests. Slimy.

If you CHOSE ←THIS:

You'll bust a move with a booby—a **BLUE-FOOTED BOOBY**, that is—if you head to the Galápagos Islands. These remote islands in the Pacific Ocean are home to about half of the world's blue-footed booby population, birds that are famous for the funny dance routine they perform to find mates. The males show off their blue kicks with a **HIGH-STEPPING STRUT** in hopes of attracting a female. While you're there, be sure to look for any lizards roaming the beach where the birds lay their eggs. You wouldn't want to miss your chance to see the Galápagos land iguana—it exists nowhere else in the world!

blue-footed booby

If you CHOSE ↓THAT:

If you want to play games with a **TOMATO FROG**, you'll hop all the way to Madagascar, an island where 90 percent of the plants and animals are native to nowhere else in the world. But heads up, don't mistake this red-hot amphibian for a salad ingredient. The tomato frog secretes a thick, sticky substance that can **IRRITATE** the skin, eyes, and mouth of any would-be **PREDATOR**. While not usually toxic to humans, the frog's juices can be very annoying, so maybe it's wise to hang out with one of the islands many other unique critters!

tomato frog

LET'S SEE WHAT YOUR CHOICES SAY ABOUT YOU.

DOC TALK ...

PSYCHOLOGIST DR. MATT BELLACE DISSECTS YOUR DECISIONS ...

ANALYZE THIS!

If you mostly picked **CHOOSE THIS,** you're a pretty typical person ... who just happens to enjoy the company of a Yeti or a blue-footed booby! You're open to some of the odder aspects of life, and you certainly don't judge others for who (or what!) they are, but you truly take pleasure in the simplicity of day-to-day normality. You may fear that you're boring, but don't worry, your friends count on you for your dependable and constant nature. So sure, you'll hang with a Yeti or a blue-footed booby—you're not judging!

ANALYZE THAT!

If you mostly picked **CHOOSE THAT,** you're a one-of-a-kind type of person who is drawn to the more unusual and bizarre aspects of life. When you see a person recoil at the smell of something, you lean forward for a whiff. When everyone runs screaming from a dark cave, you head inside. You love risky adventures and extreme challenges, and this type of behavior will win you many fans who are delighted to live life through your eyes. But beware, these so-called friends may encourage you to do dangerous things that could get you hurt ... or grounded.

CHAPTER 4

FEED ME!

Got the stomach grumbles? Have you spent all day thinking about cupcakes, cookies, and candy? Or perhaps something more savory, like sandwiches and cheese? Whatever your fancy, this chapter is perfect to get you geared up for your next meal. Just a heads up, there may be some food here you've never seen on the menu ...

CHOOSE THIS:

Eat **breakfast** but be **late** for **school**.

or

CHOOSE THAT:

Skip breakfast **but** be **on** time **for** school.

MUSE BEFORE YOU CHOOSE

Full belly. Mad teacher. Morning announcements are important. Daydreaming about food for three hours.

If you CHOSE ↓THIS:

Start the day off right with a nice **BOWL OF POPCORN**— wait, what? Long before boxed cereal, settlers in **COLONIAL AMERICA** ate bowls of popcorn for breakfast. Even in the late 1800s, John Harvey Kellogg—coinventor of the **CORN FLAKES** that to this day bear his name—would eat a bowl of mashed-up popcorn with a little milk and sugar. Give it a try with some fruit and yogurt on the side. Yum!

If you CHOSE THAT: ↓

You won't be tardy, but you'll probably be hungry! Studies have shown that kids who eat breakfast **BEFORE SCHOOL** have **IMPROVED CONCENTRATION** and perform better on tests. Skipping breakfast is like trying to drive a car with no fuel in the tank, so if you want to have **ENERGY FOR RECESS**, plan on waking up with enough time to sit down at the table.

Think Twice!

Pork porridge is a breakfast food from Thailand with some pretty interesting ingredients. How does blood pudding and stuffed pork intestines sound first thing in the morning?

CHOOSE

THIS:

Feast on funky fruit from planet Earth.

square watermelon

or

CHOOSE

THAT:

Get your **vitamins** from **alien** veggies.

MUSE
BEFORE YOU
CHOOSE

Not your average apple. Outrageous oranges. Extraterrestrial eggplant. Spaced-out sprouts.

If you CHOSE **THIS:** ⬇

If you like your **FRUIT FUNKY,** you should see the watermelons in Japan. They come in all shapes and sizes! Square watermelons are especially useful because they are **STACKABLE** on grocery store shelves. They get their unique shape from special boxes that mold them as the fruits grow. Some fetch **HUNDREDS OF DOLLARS!** Who says it doesn't pay to play with your food?

If you CHOSE ⬇**THAT:**

That green on your plate is out of this world ... literally! NASA's Vegetable Production System—known as **VEGGIE**—grows lettuce 248 miles (400 km) above Earth's soil. But don't get the salad dressing out just yet. Veggie is still in an experimental phase, and many tests need to be performed for bacteria and cleanliness before astronauts can eat the produce. It costs about **$10,000** to send **1 POUND** (454 g) of food from Earth to the **SPACE STATION,** so growing food there could save a lot of money. And because space can get a little lonely at times, **NASA** also believes tending plants in a garden could provide a form of therapy for the crew.

CHOOSE THIS:

Eat 70 hot dogs in 10 minutes.

or

CHOOSE THAT:

Eat 50 pancakes in 10 minutes.

MUSE BEFORE YOU CHOOSE

Impress everyone in the cafeteria. Condiment overload. Syrupy sugar rush. Bloated after breakfast.

If you CHOSE THIS:

You've got quite the appetite, don't you? Perhaps competitive eating may be of interest. Check out **NATHAN'S FAMOUS INTERNATIONAL HOT DOG EATING CONTEST,** which is held every Fourth of July in Coney Island, New York, U.S.A. Started in 1916 when Nathan Handwerker opened his hot dog restaurant, the event draws some 40,000 fans each year. You'll have to eat **70 HOT DOGS** (and buns) in **10 MINUTES** if you want to go down in history. Joey "Jaws" Chestnut broke the world record in 2013 by eating 69!

That's Gross!

One of the most disgusting eating records is held by Oleg Zhornitskiy. He ate four 32-ounce bowls of mayonnaise in 8 minutes! Yuck!

If you CHOSE THAT:

You'd think chowing down on **50 PANCAKES** in **10 MINUTES** would get you a world record, but you'd actually only tie for one! Competitive eating champion Patrick Bertoletti already holds the record, among many others. He has gobbled **47 DOUGHNUTS** in 5 minutes, and swallowed **9.17 POUNDS** (4.16 kg) of **BLUEBERRY PIE** in 8 minutes without using his hands! There's a reason Bertoletti holds more eating records than anyone else—his stomach is unmatched!

CHOOSE
THIS:
Fast food

ostriches

or

CHOOSE
THAT:
Slow food

MUSE
BEFORE YOU
CHOOSE

More time to do other things. May not be as nutritious. Savor the flavor. Long waits.

If you CHOSE ⬇THIS:

The **OSTRICH** may be fast—clocking in at **43 MILES AN HOUR** (70 kph)—but it's *slowly* moving toward your dinner plate. Ostrich ranches are popping up all over the world as the bird's meat grows in popularity. What's crazy is that ostrich meat tastes more like beef than poultry. It's roughly 90 percent **LOWER IN FAT** than beef, while also high in protein, iron, and calcium. An added bonus: Ostrich is usually raised organically. This bird may be on its way to becoming America's favorite **DINNERTIME DISH.**

If you CHOSE THAT:⬇

You like taking time to enjoy your meal? Well, you're like the **KOALA,** which keeps its food in its digestive system for very long periods of time. The koala lives on a diet of **EUCALYPTUS LEAVES,** which are low in nutrition. In order to get as much energy as possible from the plant, koalas are equipped with an extra-long digestive organ called a **CECUM** that breaks down the fibers into substances that can be absorbed over time. The downside to slow food is that pretty much everything else must be slow too—koalas **SLEEP UP TO 20 HOURS** a day!

◀ koala

CHOOSE **THIS:**

Munch on cheese that squirms.

or

CHOOSE **THAT:**

Chew on seafood that wriggles.

MUSE BEFORE YOU CHOOSE

Daily dose of dairy. Weird texture. High in protein. Catching it with your fork!

74

If you CHOSE ⬇THIS:

Prepare your taste buds for *CASU MARZU*, a cheese famous for what's writhing in every bite—**MAGGOTS!** Casu marzu is made from the curds of sheep's milk and is left outside for months so flies will come by and lay their eggs in it. The eggs hatch into larvae that feast on the rotting cheese. When it's good and soft, spread some on a cracker and feel the maggots **SQUIRM IN YOUR MOUTH.** You'll have to travel to Europe for a taste, because it's banned in the U.S.A. Chewing maggots doesn't necessarily kill them, which means they could make a new home inside your tummy!

If you CHOSE THAT:

You're going to chew, chew, chew if you're eating **RAW OCTOPUS!** *Sannakji* is a Korean dish made from octopus that is cut up and served immediately to the eater while the tentacles are still wriggling on the plate. The **TENTACLES' SUCTION CUPS** will stick to your mouth and teeth, giving you a strange (yet satisfying?) sensation. But beware the choking risks associated with sannakji. Amateur eaters are advised to chew carefully, because raw octopus arms have been known to **CLIMB BACK UP** the throat!

▲ octopus

CHOOSE THIS:

Spend all your savings on a grand dessert.

CHOOSE THAT:

Save your money and have a simple treat.

MUSE
BEFORE YOU
CHOOSE

Dine in style.
You'll be broke!
Cash on hand.
Underwhelming.

If you CHOSE THIS:

You can fork over **$1,000** for the world's most expensive **ICE-CREAM SUNDAE** at Serendipity 3 in New York City. The Golden Opulence Sundae has fancy vanilla ice cream covered in 23-carat edible gold leaf. It's then drizzled with one of the world's most expensive chocolates and topped with candied fruit, **GOLD-COVERED ALMONDS**, chocolate truffles, marzipan cherries, and a bowl of Grande Passion caviar (yes, fish eggs!), and served with an **18-CARAT GOLD SPOON**. (Nope, you don't get to keep the spoon.)

Choice Nugget

Think $30 is a bit much to pay for a fortune cookie? What if it was covered in chocolate and candy and was bigger than both your hands? These GIANT treats from Fancy Fortune Cookies in Indiana, U.S.A., are as big as they come!

If you CHOSE THAT:

You won't have to spend a fortune for a taste of *JALEBI,* a popular sweet found in southern Asia and North Africa. It's made by deep-frying flour batter into circular shapes and then soaking them in syrup. This tasty treat has a chewy texture with a **CRYSTALLIZED SUGAR** coating and can be eaten hot or cold. Jalebi is widely known as "the celebration sweet of India" because you are likely to find it at any happy occasion, from birthdays to graduations, and it is **INEXPENSIVE** to make. You won't be disappointed that you chose to save your money for something more lasting than dessert!

THIS:

Set your mouth on fire.

or

Carolina Reaper chili pepper

CHOOSE

THAT:

Get your tongue twisted.

MUSE BEFORE YOU CHOOSE

Feel the heat. Sweating. Tangy taste. Funny photos.

If you CHOSE
⬇THIS:

You'll set your mouth ablaze if you try a **CAROLINA REAPER,** the world's hottest chili pepper. This tongue torcher is high in **CAPSAICIN,** the natural chemical in chili peppers that creates a burning sensation in the tissues of mammals, including humans. You'll feel the power behind this one-of-a-kind chili—it's about **100 TIMES HOTTER** than the jalapeño. Good luck trying to cool off your taste buds!

If you CHOSE
⬇THAT:

Your tongue will do flips if you taste **SUPERSOUR CANDIES** like Warheads and Sweet Tarts. Treats as sour as these are very **HIGH IN ACID,** which leaves the mouth feeling burned if eaten in large amounts. Be warned! Your dentist won't be happy if you're gobbling too many tart candies at once—their acids will eat through your teeth!

LET'S SEE WHAT **YOUR CHOICES** SAY **ABOUT YOU.**

DOC TALK ...

PSYCHOLOGIST DR. MATT BELLACE DISSECTS YOUR DECISIONS ...

ANALYZE THIS!

If you mostly picked **CHOOSE THIS,** good news! You don't worry about what other people think of you. You're an adventurous person with a taste for the unconventional, and you don't stress about how your choices make you look to others. Some might describe you as impulsive, which can be good and bad. On the plus side, you're not bogged down by social conventions and can think outside the box. But your reckless behavior can also lead to consequences. Keep doing your thing, but remember to ask for help when you've bitten off more than you can chew.

ANALYZE THAT!

If you mostly picked **CHOOSE THAT,** you're a practical decision-maker, especially when it comes to gastronomic adventures. You realize that skipping a meal to get to school doesn't mean you can't sneak a snack in before algebra class, and that even if veggies are grown in space, you still have to eat them to get to dessert! Being practical has its benefits, but remember not to knock something until you try it. Who knows, you just might love the very thing you swore you'd hate.

CHAPTER 5

HEAD to TOE

Take one last look in the mirror because very soon you're not going to recognize yourself. This chapter is all about extra headgear, foot extensions, and other body oddities that may not look so pretty but could come in very handy. It's time for an EXTREME makeover!

CHOOSE
THIS:
Your **earwax** tells a **story.**

or

CHOOSE
THAT:
Your **poop** serves as transportation for **others.**

MUSE BEFORE YOU CHOOSE

Easy bedtime reading. Clogs your hearing. Handy vehicle. Smelly passengers.

84

mother humpback whale and calf

If you CHOSE ⬇THIS:

It's not a story you'd want to hear right before eating, but **WHALE EARWAX** has been found to tell a tale about the animal's life. A layer of wax is deposited every **SIX MONTHS** into a wad called an **EARPLUG.** And since the whale can't clean it out, the wax builds up over its lifetime. After the whale has passed away, scientists can dissect the earwax layers to determine if the whale was exposed to toxins and pollutants in the water at different stages of its life or if the whale experienced **STRESS** and shifts in its maturity, like moving from childhood to **ADOLESCENCE.** It's one gross story with a cool ending!

If you CHOSE ⬇THAT:

All aboard the poop train! That's what plant seeds would say to the **TAMBAQUI FISH** found in South America. Tambaquis are closely related to the piranha, but they don't have an appetite for flesh—they're more interested in eating fruits that have fallen into the water and the seeds they contain. As the fish swim around looking for more food, they **CARRY THE SEEDS IN THEIR BELLIES** to different parts of the jungle and then poop them out. That's good news for plants that want to spread their seeds as **FAR AS POSSIBLE**— they've got a fishy belly as a car pool!

tambaqui fish

CHOOSE THIS:

You have a **long** neck like a **giraffe**.

or

CHOOSE THAT:

You can **turn** your **head** completely **around** like an **owl**.

MUSE BEFORE YOU CHOOSE

See the show better at a concert. Stick out in a crowd. Fun party trick. Nobody can sneak up on you.

If you CHOSE ↓THIS:

It turns out you don't have to be an animal to mimic a **GIRAFFE**. The **KAYAN WOMEN** of Thailand wear brass coils intended to lengthen their necks over time as a statement of beauty. However, these **RINGS** don't actually add inches to the neck itself—their weight slowly pushes down the collar bone and shoulders, giving the appearance that the neck is longer. The women wear them from the age of five and rarely take them off.

giraffe

If you CHOSE THAT:↓

An owl can't really turn its head full circle, otherwise it would fall off, but it can go a remarkable **270 DEGREES**. By contrast, humans can only go 180 degrees. This neck ability allows owls to look completely over their shoulder. What's amazing is that doing this doesn't cut off **BLOOD SUPPLY** to the brain or damage arteries. That's because owls have special **AIR POCKETS** in their neck bones that act as cushions for the arteries as they twist.

long-eared owl

Think Twice!

The sauropods— a group of dinosaurs known for their enormous size—had superlong necks made of 60% air.

CHOOSE THIS:

Your nose is a proboscis.

CHOOSE THAT:

You don't have a nose.

MUSE BEFORE YOU CHOOSE

Easy to grab things when your hands are full. Weird-looking school pics. No sneezing! How will you smell what's for dinner?

IF YOU CHOSE THIS:

Having a **PROBOSCIS** means you have a pretty big nose! The term is used for animal noses that may be long or flexible. Take the **SAIGA ANTELOPE**. It may look like a creature from *Star Wars*, but it's actually a living species here on planet Earth. Its funky nose has an internal structure of bone, hair, and mucous-secreting glands that allow it to **FILTER DUST** from the air in summertime. That's quite a helpful smeller!

saiga antelope

IF YOU CHOSE THAT:

Sniffing stuff isn't very useful if you're a **BOTTLENOSE DOLPHIN**. Even though dolphins are air-breathing mammals like us, it is believed they have no sense of smell because there are **NO OLFACTORY LOBES** in their brains. These lobes are the parts that transmit smell information from the nose to the brain for interpretation, and apparently dolphins have evolved to not need them. Sure, you won't be able to get a whiff of a delicious dinner cooking, but if you're a dolphin you won't need to. Raw fish please!

bottlenose dolphin

Choice Nugget

Butterflies have a proboscis that they uncurl to sip nectar from flowers.

CHOOSE **THIS:**

You move **slowly,** but your armor is **hard** as **a rock.**

or

CHOOSE **THAT:**

Your **armor** is **spongy,** but **you** can **get** around.

MUSE BEFORE YOU CHOOSE Feel like a knight. Panic in bathroom emergencies. Flexibility. Spongy defense.

90

If you CHOSE ⬇THIS:

Venezuelan pebble toad

It's a rock-and-roll life for the **VENEZUELAN PEBBLE TOAD**—*literally.* When confronted by a predator, the clever toad folds its arms and legs under its body, tightens its muscles, and then **HURLS ITSELF** down the mountainside. Just when a predator is about to pounce, the toad bounces out of reach! Because the amphibian is so small—about **AN INCH IN LENGTH** (2.5 cm)—the forces of impact as it hits the ground are too tiny to inflict bodily damage. The only problem is these toads are terrible swimmers and hoppers. They can only hop an inch at a time!

If you CHOSE ⬇THAT:

Defense doesn't have to be restricting when you've got the **SQUISHY BODY ARMOR** of a **SEAHORSE.** This creature has unique plates on its tail that slide past one another, allowing it to twist and bend around seaweed and coral while still **PROTECTING THE SPINE** within. Many of the seahorse's predators—crabs, turtles, fish, rays—capture their prey by crushing them in their claws or beaks. So, flexible armor like this makes it a little harder for the seahorse to get eaten while making it **EASY TO GET AROUND.**

seahorse

CHOOSE THIS:

You have **extremely** long **horns.**

or

CHOOSE THAT:

You have **extremely** long **teeth.**

MUSE BEFORE YOU CHOOSE   Bullies beware! Heavy headgear. Vampire tendencies. More brushing.

If you CHOSE ⬇ THIS:

You might give yourself a **HEADACHE** if you've got horns like **LURCH THE BULL,** who held the world record for the biggest set. His horns were nearly **8 FEET** (2.4 m) long from tip to tip, were **38 INCHES AROUND** (1 m), and weighed **100 POUNDS** (45 kg) each. Lurch was an **ANKOLE-WATUSI STEER,** a breed of cattle known for its horn size that is revered among many peoples in Africa. Despite their weight, horns like Lurch's could come in handy when defending against predators.

Lurch the bull, Ankole-Watusi steer

If you CHOSE THAT: ⬇

Your dentist might give you a weird look if your teeth are as big as a **WALRUS'S!** These blubbery creatures live mostly in the **ARCTIC CIRCLE,** where having long tusks can be especially useful. Walruses use their **CANINES**—which grow up to 3 feet (1 m) long—to haul their massive bodies out of the cold water and to break **BREATHING HOLES** in the ice from below. Walrus canine teeth grow throughout their lives, so sometimes scientists measure their length to determine how old a walrus is. If a walrus loses a tooth, it doesn't grow back!

walrus

Think Twice!

The rhinoceros is the only animal to have horns on top of its nose.

CHOOSE THIS:

You eat food grown on your own body.

yeti crab

or

CHOOSE THAT:

You eat food off of someone else's body.

MUSE BEFORE YOU CHOOSE

Snacking is easy. Is it sanitary? You have to ask permission first. You don't have to carry around the weight.

If you CHOSE THIS:

Dinner is always close at hand if you're a **YETI CRAB**. The hairs on this crustacean's long arms support colonies of **BACTERIA** that live off of the mineral-rich water spewing from **HYDROTHERMAL VENTS**. Whenever the crab gets hungry, it just nibbles on its arm hairs! These mostly color-less crabs live at depths of more than 7,800 feet (2,377 m), where gases spurting from below the Earth's surface heat the surrounding water to temperatures you'd find in the **TROPICS**. When you've always got snacks on your body like these guys, there's no reason to ever be in a crabby mood!

If you CHOSE THAT:

Your friends will be spic-and-span if you're a **BLUESTREAK CLEANER WRASSE**. These brightly colored fish—found mostly in the Indian and Pacific Oceans—**EAT PARASITES** off the scales of larger fish. Wrasses usually have a "uniform" they wear to send would-be predators one simple message: "Hey, don't eat me! I'm here to help!" The **CLEANER FISH UNIFORM** consists of a bright base color with a dark side stripe and patches of blue and yellow. The client fish assumes a position that lets them know it's safe, and that's when the wrasse goes to town nibbling. Once finished, the big fish swims away all tidied up, and the wrasse has a belly full of yummy parasites! *Mmmm!*

titan triggerfish being cleaned by a bluestreak cleaner wrasse

CHOOSE THIS:

Your feet **launch** **you** into the **air** like a **kangaroo.**

kangaroo

or

CHOOSE THAT:

Your **feet** launch you **through** the **water** like a **mermaid.**

MUSE BEFORE YOU CHOOSE Slam dunks are easy. Clumsy dancing. Outswim sharks. No more dog paddle!

96

If you CHOSE ⬇THIS:

Going for a jog in your neighborhood will never be the same when you wear your **KANGOO JUMPS** running boots. These kicks will launch you a few inches off the ground with each step, similar to the feet of those bouncy **MARSUPIALS** in the **AUSTRALIAN OUTBACK.** Kangaroos are naturally equipped with a spring in their step, but we humans are sometimes left achy and sore from a jog. Kangoo Jumps make running easier on the body by reducing the impact of each step on the hard ground.

If you CHOSE ⬇THAT:

Slide your feet into these cool fins and you'll swim like the **LITTLE MERMAID.** Eric Ducharme—an artist in Florida, U.S.A.—provides mermaid lovers with custom-made, one-of-a-kind tails. Each fin is made to the swimmer's body measurements out of **LATEX, SILICONE,** or **SPANDEX,** and is painted in shimmering colors. Wearing it might feel awkward at first, but with the right flick of your feet, you'll launch through the water like a mythical sea creature. Ready to give one a test-dive?

Think Twice!

In 1980, Joe Bowen walked from California to Kentucky, U.S.A., on stilts—that's over 3,000 miles (4,828 km)!

97

LET'S SEE WHAT **YOUR CHOICES** SAY **ABOUT YOU.**

DOC TALK ...

PSYCHOLOGIST DR. MATT BELLACE DISSECTS YOUR DECISIONS ...

ANALYZE THIS!

If you mostly picked **CHOOSE THIS,** you have an independent personality and are extremely self-sufficient. You dream of living off the land and creating your own lifestyle. This applies to filtering your own air, growing your own food, and fighting your own battles. You also value your health, which explains the body armor and fascination with earwax. The only problem is that sometimes you can be *too* self-sufficient. It's okay to rely on others—after all, social support is a key to happiness. Remember to foster your friendships, too, and you'll be unstoppable!

ANALYZE THAT!

If you mostly picked **CHOOSE THAT,** then congratulations, because the world needs more people like you! You're a social person who wants to make a difference for others. Whether you're dispersing seeds through your poop or cleaning parasites off of other creatures, you truly love making the world a better place. However, being too selfless can also be a problem. Being kind is wonderful, but be sure not to let others take advantage of you. After all, you're important, too!

CHAPTER 6

COOL TECH!

The future is here, folks. Choose between these state-of-the-art options and prepare to be wowed. From flying cars to super-cool gadgets, this chapter is about all the technology we use and where it's going next!

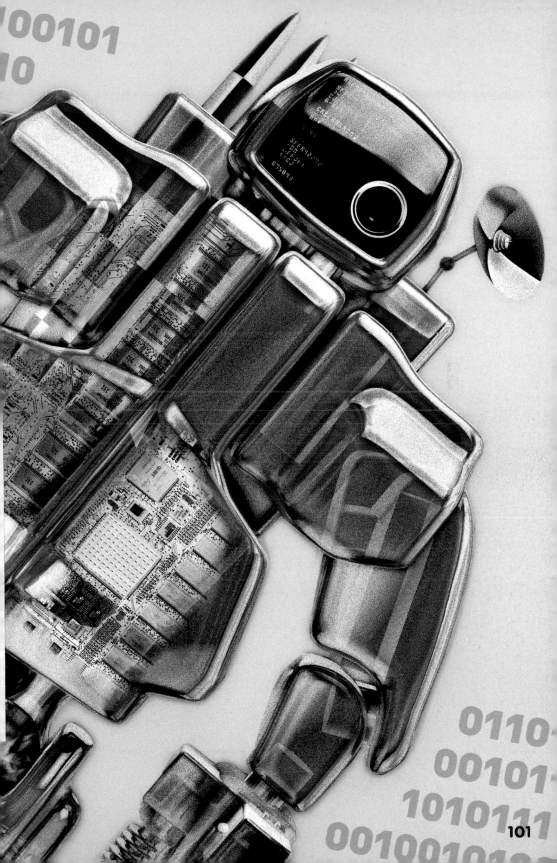

CHOOSE

THIS:

"Hi, toilet!" says the bathtub.

or

CHOOSE

THAT:

"Open sesame!" says your finger.

Intelligent home. Bathroom gossip. Magic words. Instant access.

If you CHOSE THIS: ⬇

You've heard of a smartphone, but how about a smart doorknob? Or a smart refrigerator? Well, those gadgets aren't far away from your daily life, according to a popular movement among tech geeks. It's called the "INTERNET OF THINGS," which predicts there will be more than 50 billion objects connected to the World Wide Web by the YEAR 2020. That's more than six objects for every one person on the planet! These devices will keep track of how you live your life and will be able to communicate object to object WITHOUT any human involvement. Your smart bathtub will know the precise temperature you like your water, and your toilet will analyze your diet based on, well, what you leave behind!

If you CHOSE ⬇THAT:

SCANNING FINGERPRINTS isn't just for the police anymore—it's about to be for you, too! Each human fingerprint has a unique arrangement of ridges and valleys, which makes it a perfect way to secure access to your computer, home, and anything else you can possibly think of. Say goodbye to all those PASSWORDS floating around in your head, because scanning fingerprints has many positives. You can't guess a fingerprint pattern like you can a password, and you can't forget it since it's connected to your hand. When you place your finger on a scanner, the light sensor takes a picture. A computer then looks for tiny distinctive features and compares them to your previous scans. Only then will the device UNLOCK.

CHOOSE THIS:

Your car is also an airplane.

or

CHOOSE THAT:

Your car is also a submarine.

MUSE BEFORE YOU CHOOSE

Autographs from Superman. Turbulence. Autographs from SpongeBob. Limited oxygen supply.

Transition flying car

If you CHOSE ⬇THIS:

Your friends will be impressed when you show up at school in your **FLYING CAR!** That's right, a company called Terrafugia has made the future a reality with the **TRANSITION**, a car that converts to an airplane in just under 60 seconds. All you need is $279,000 and a pilot's license and you can own one of the first models currently in production. You can also look forward to Terrafugia's next model, the TF-X, which will be able to take off vertically **WITHOUT A RUNWAY.**

If you CHOSE THAT:⬇

Take a dive in a sQuba, the world's first truly **SUBMERSIBLE CAR.** This electric sports car has a diving depth of 33 feet (10 m). It's equipped with **THREE MOTORS** in the rear: one for propulsion on land and two to drive propellers under-water. There are two addi-tional motors in the front that provide maneu-verability while submerged. On land, the **SQUBA** will cruise up to 75 miles an hour (120 kph) and is equipped with **LASER TECHNOLOGY** that allows it to drive on its own.

sQuba submersible car

Think Twice!

A "submarine car" was used in the 1977 James Bond film *The Spy Who Loved Me*, but it was not equipped with wheels and could not drive on land. Even so, it still sold at auction in September 2013 for nearly $1 million.

105

CHOOSE
THIS:
You have a spacecraft in your pocket.

or

CHOOSE
THAT:
Your friends are holograms.

MUSE
BEFORE YOU
CHOOSE

Vacations on Mars. Crashing into an asteroid. See your friends in 3-D when they're far away. Feel like you're in *Star Wars*.

If you CHOSE ⬇THIS:

As early as 2015, you could own a **PERSONALIZED SPACECRAFT** small enough to fit in your pocket. A company has developed CD-shaped discs called "Scouts" that are about three inches (7.6 cm) across and as thin as a **SHEET OF PAPER**. They cost as low as $154, allowing everyday people to take part in space exploration. The Scouts will be loaded onto a rocket set to launch in 2015. Your disc (and many others) will be released into space and will fall back to Earth, **COLLECTING DATA** you can analyze upon their return. Don't worry if you miss the first rocket launch another batch of Scouts will be launched to the moon in 2016!

If you CHOSE ⬇THAT:

HOLOGRAMS like the ones you've seen in *Star Wars* may be just around the corner. A pyramid-shaped product called HOLHO utilizes mirrors to display moving **THREE-DIMENSIONAL** images from your smartphone. You record pictures of something—like your baseball glove—and the app will convert them into images that can be shown as a hologram. Some experts say the technology still has a ways to go, but there are many companies working on **SIMILAR DEVICES**. Who knows, you might be able to display a friend in 3-D sooner than you think!

CHOOSE THIS:

Never wait more than a minute to play with your friends.

or

CHOOSE THAT:

Never wait more than a minute for pizza delivery.

MUSE BEFORE YOU CHOOSE

No more boredom. Goodbye, loneliness! Cravings are easily satisfied. Food is always hot!

IF YOU CHOSE THIS:

Your friends are always close at hand, thanks to **PHOTO BOOTHS** that will turn you and your buddies into **3-D PRINTED FIGURINES**. You step into the booth, and a ring of scanners takes pictures of your body from all angles. A computer then puts these images together and produces a 3-D model printed in **PLASTIC**, up to 14 inches (35 cm) tall. That way, if you ever get lonely you don't have to wait for anyone to come over. Instead, you can play with **ACTION FIGURES** of your friends—but they probably won't be as fun as the real thing!

IF YOU CHOSE THAT:

Feast your eyes on this: a **3-D FOOD PRINTER** that "prints" real, edible pizza. Developed for NASA, the printer will help feed astronauts during long space missions far away from fresh ingredients. The machine prints a **LAYER OF DOUGH** that bakes onto a heated plate, followed by a tomato base. Last, a yummy-sounding "protein layer" is applied, which comes from animals, milk, or plants. It may not be the delivery you're used to, but this is pizza you won't have to wait for!

EAT!

CHOOSE THIS:
Your car **window** is a **touch** screen.

or

CHOOSE THAT:
Your bathroom **mirror** is a **touch** screen.

MUSE BEFORE YOU CHOOSE Boredom buster for long road trips. Distracting. Check messages while brushing your teeth. Spend more time getting ready.

If you CHOSE THIS: ⬇

DRAWING IN MOTION

SHOW OTHER CAR'S DRAWINGS

ZOOM IN AND CAPTURE ENVIRONMENT

Road trips will never be boring if your car has Toyota's new concept called "WINDOW TO THE WORLD." This technology turns the average car window into a touch screen, allowing you to interact with the scenery as it passes by. See a tree on the horizon? TAP ON THE GLASS to find out how far away it is. Want to know what kind of tree it is? Zoom in and look it up on Google. With your window to the world, you'll be thoroughly entertained, even on your ride to school!

If you CHOSE ⬇ THAT:

You'll see more than your reflection if you have a POSH iMirror in your bathroom. While brushing your teeth, you could see the DAY'S WEATHER FORECAST, news headlines, and even emails and text messages. But don't worry about your little brother seeing messages from your friends—FACIAL RECOGNITION features will be built into the mirror so only *you* are able to access your information. Just tap on the glass and watch your favorite TV SHOW as you get ready for your day. Fixing your hair just got a lot more techy, didn't it?

CHOOSE THIS:

Take a robot **dog** for a **walk.**

or

CHOOSE THAT:

Have **your plants** pollinated by **robot** bees.

MUSE BEFORE YOU CHOOSE No poop-scooping! Not as cuddly. No stings! No honey.

If you CHOSE
⬇THIS:

Sorry but you won't be playing fetch with **BIGDOG**, the rough-terrain **ROBOT** developed by a company near Boston, Massachusetts, for the United States government. Roughly the size of a large dog like a Great Dane, BigDog weighs 240 pounds (109 kg). It can walk, climb, and **CARRY LOADS** up to 340 pounds (154 kg). The robot was developed to **HELP SOLDIERS** carry supplies, allowing them to conserve their physical energy. Imagine taking this pup out on a leash!

BigDog robot

If you CHOSE
⬇THAT:

Don't be surprised if you look out in the garden and find a tiny speck of metal buzzing among the flowers. **ROBOBEES** are being developed at Harvard University to address a worst-case scenario—if our (real) honeybees are no longer around to pollinate crops. Bees have been undergoing **COLONY COLLAPSE DISORDER,** which occurs when seemingly healthy bees abandon their hives and never return. Scientists suspect that pesticides, parasitic mites, and a virus may be to blame for their disappearances. If bees are no longer around, you'd have to say goodbye to many of your favorite fruits and vegetables, which is why RoboBees may serve as **REPLACEMENT POLLINATORS** in the future.

RoboBees

CHOOSE THIS:

Odorless farts

or

CHOOSE THAT:

Bad breath alerts

MUSE BEFORE YOU CHOOSE

Bring on the bean burritos! No more awkward elevator rides. *Mmmm*, garlic bread. No embarrassing looks from your crush!

If you CHOSE
THIS:

You can say goodbye to stinkers if you're wearing **SHREDDIES**. This high-tech **UNDERWEAR** is designed to stop smells from your backside before they reach the nostrils of the people around you. They feel and look like normal (boring) underwear, but Shreddies are made with a panel of activated **CARBON** that absorbs **PUNGENT AROMAS**. The carbon is reactivated with each washing, so you can get the same odor-free effect time and time again. So go ahead and eat that burrito at lunch! You'll be sitting in class with a big smile on your face, and no one will know why.

If you CHOSE THAT:

Everybody gets **HALITOSIS**—bad breath—from time to time, but we often don't realize it until a friend curls their nose once we've said hello. A **BAD BREATH** detection app for your smartphone is currently in development that will send a notification that you could use a mint. The chip will have about 2,000 sensors to detect smells in the air. Now you won't have to worry about **SMELLY SIGHS** around your friends (and crushes).

115

LET'S SEE WHAT **YOUR CHOICES** SAY **ABOUT YOU.**

DOC TALK ...

PSYCHOLOGIST DR. MATT BELLACE DISSECTS YOUR DECISIONS ...

ANALYZE
THIS!

If you mostly picked **CHOOSE THIS,** you have a laid-back personality that some people might mistake for laziness. But you're not lazy; you're innovative! You like finding clever ways to make life easier, and you embrace cool new technologies. Fart-filtering underwear? Check! In fact, you may even create your own inventions to make life run more smoothly. Just be sure that you can muster up the motivation to face difficult challenges when they come along, and you're on your way to an awesome, tech-savvy future.

ANALYZE
THAT!

If you mostly picked **CHOOSE THAT,** you're an old-fashioned, do-it-yourself kind of person. Sure, technology can be useful, but who wants it to run their lives? You'd much rather be the one in control, and you're probably great at camping! You'll be just fine if computers ever try to take over the world ... but until then, you'll be expected to know how to use at least one or two software programs, so it's probably a good idea to brush up on your computer skills in addition to all those awesome life skills you already have.

CHAPTER 7

DREAM JOBS

What do you want to be when you grow up? With an infinite number of possibilities, that can be a difficult question to answer. Doctor? Astronaut? Or maybe something a little different, like professional feet sniffer (it exists!)? This chapter is all about the career of your dreams, so think about each option carefully. We wouldn't want you stuck with the job of your nightmares.

CHOOSE
THIS:

Be a **code-breaker** in the **safety** of a library.

Voynich manuscript

or

CHOOSE
THAT:

Solve a **mystery** chasing **bad** guys **on** the **run.**

MUSE BEFORE YOU CHOOSE

Always hearing *"Shhhh!"* Paper cuts. Adrenaline pumping. Car chases.

If you CHOSE ⬇THIS:

You should consider becoming a PALEOGRAPHER—someone who studies ancient writing and books—and take a stab at reading the Voynich manuscript. Written some 500 years ago, this book continues to mystify researchers and book collectors alike, because, well, up to now no one has been able to read it! The text is in a script unlike any other known language, and even the best code-breakers haven't detected any patterns in its symbols. With beautiful images of PLANTS and HUMAN FIGURES, it might be a MEDIEVAL BOOK OF POTIONS. Sounds like something Harry Potter's Professor Snape would approve of.

If you CHOSE THAT:⬇

WATCH OUT CRIMINALS! There's a new police detective in town. Detectives gather facts and collect evidence of possible crimes, but there are a few things you have to accomplish before you begin your first investigation. Most detectives start out as police officers and must graduate from a training academy. According to the U.S. Department of Labor, some of the qualities a police officer is expected to have are:

EMPATHY You'll need to understand the perspectives of a wide variety of people and have the desire to help them.
COMMUNICATION SKILLS You'll have to speak with people when gathering facts about a crime and you'll have to give details in writing.
GOOD JUDGMENT You'll need to figure out the best way to solve all kinds of problems very quickly.
LEADERSHIP SKILLS Everyone in your community will look to you to set the example. You'll need to know how to behave so people will follow and respect you.
PERCEPTIVENESS You'll need to understand why people act a certain way, much like a psychologist would, so you always stay one step ahead of a criminal.
STRENGTH AND STAMINA Sometimes officers and detectives have to chase down bad guys. Being in good physical shape is very important to get into the training academy and to keep up with the daily rigors of the job.

CHOOSE **THIS:**

Your **office** looks like a **playground.**

or

CHOOSE **THAT:**

Your **uniform** is a **wet suit.**

MUSE BEFORE YOU CHOOSE

Recess everyday! Sounds too good to be true. Underwater meetings. Heavy scuba tanks.

If you CHOSE ⬇THIS:

YouTube headquarters, California, U.S.A.

Head to San Bruno, California, U.S.A., and apply for a job at **YOUTUBE**. YouTube's headquarters features a three-person slide for employees to have a little fun, in addition to a **MINIATURE GOLF COURSE, CLIMBING WALL,** and numerous **SNACK BARS.** The staff know how to have a good time, but when it comes to their work they're very committed. One hundred hours of video content is uploaded to YouTube every minute, and more than one billion unique users visit the website every month. Keeping a site that big up and running takes a lot of hard work ... and, apparently, playground equipment.

If you CHOSE THAT:⬇

Strap on your fins because you're going for a swim—with **SHARKS!** If you're a **DIVE SAFETY OFFICER** like Jen Meeks at the Newport Aquarium in Kentucky, U.S.A., you'll need to be comfortable getting in the water with some of the world's largest predators. "The most surprising thing is how smart they are," says Meeks. "The sharks have individual personalities. We have a **SAND TIGER SHARK** named Big Al who is very curious. He's always checking out new things in his tank." Part of Meeks's job is to train a crew of volunteers how to safely clean the tanks without disturbing the animals. "We're very **RESPECTFUL** to the sharks. We make sure we don't accidentally kick them with our fins or **SPLASH AROUND** too much. As long as we're respectful, they don't bother us."

Think Twice!

In 2013, British university student Seb Smith was selected to be a waterslide tester for a resort company. More than 2,000 people applied for the opportunity to ride and rate waterslides at resorts around the world.

123

CHOOSE THIS:

You have a great sense of taste.

or

CHOOSE THAT:

You have an excellent sense of smell.

MUSE BEFORE YOU CHOOSE

Fabulous flavors.
Playful palate.
Fragrant aromas.
Stinky fumes.

IF YOU CHOSE THIS:

It might take awhile for your tongue to get used to its new job if you **EAT DOG FOOD** for a living. Since pups can't tell us if they like food, we humans must taste the canine cuisine for ourselves! Professional **DOG-FOOD TASTER** Mark Gooley of Australia told *Perth Now*, "If you wouldn't put it in your mouth, don't you dare expect your dog to eat it." As the owner of a pet food company, Gooley has high standards on behalf of his pooches. "I want [the food] to be **SOFT** in the mouth and I want it to be an **ENJOYABLE EXPERIENCE** for the dog." Now, go off and enjoy your kibbles and bits!

IF YOU CHOSE THAT:

Get ready to flare those nostrils if you decide to become a professional **FART SMELLER.** Yes, that's right, there are actually people who get paid to smell farts. But the job's not just about taking whiffs of stinky **AROMAS.** Smellers are thought to be able to identify health issues based on odors— wickedly stinky farts could indicate bacterial **INFECTION** in a patient's intestines. You'll also be expected to measure the amount of gas expelled with each fart, because big blowers could mean someone's eating too much fiber, while wimpy whispers could mean someone's backed up. It's more scientific than you might think, so be prepared to pass a **SMELL RECOGNITION TEST** if you decide to pursue this scent-tastic career!

Choice Nugget

There's no reason you have to restrict yourself to smelling human farts for a living—you could specialize in cow farts instead! These professional sniffers try to detect abnormalities in a cow's diet by breathing in its backside gusts.

CHOOSE **THIS:**

Spend *your* **day** sleeping like a **sloth.**

or

CHOOSE **THAT:**

Spend *your* **day** monkeying around.

MUSE
BEFORE YOU
CHOOSE

Lazy living. Sweet dreams. All-you-can-eat bananas. Poop fights.

If you CHOSE ⬇THIS:

No need to worry about getting in trouble for snoozing on the job if you're a **PROFESSIONAL SLEEPER**. Even though catching *zzz*'s for a living sounds too good to be true, some sleeping gigs are better than others. For example, in 2013 a hotel in Finland hired a sleeper to **TEST OUT** its rooms and **BLOG** about them for 35 days. That job would be a pretty good setup.

If you CHOSE THAT:⬇

You may work with monkeys if you become a **PRIMATOLOGIST**, but you'll hardly be monkeying around! Studying nonhuman primates like **CHIMPS** and **APES** can be serious work, mainly because the extreme conditions of the tropics where the animals live can be very dangerous for humans. Diseases and wild animals are some of the threats you may face out in the field. But Bethan Morgan, a primatologist who has lived and worked in **CENTRAL AFRICA**, told *Nature Education* that the rewards outweigh the risks. "Life in the field ... is intense," says Morgan. "But overall, the joy I get from simply being in the forest ... more than compensates for the downsides to my work."

common squirrel monkey

CHOOSE
THIS:
Come up with some catchy tunes.

or

CHOOSE
THAT:
Create sculptures out of toys.

MUSE BEFORE YOU CHOOSE Hear your music on the radio. Songs get stuck in your head. Play all day! See your work in a museum.

If you CHOSE ⬇ THIS:

Your name will be in flashing lights if you write **BROADWAY MUSICALS** for a living. Benj Pasek and Justin Paul, the Tony-nominated composer-songwriter duo behind *A Christmas Story* and *James and the Giant Peach*, say it's the coolest job in the world if you like **MUSIC** and **STORYTELLING**. "The best part of writing musicals is when you get to dream something in your mind and then watch the actors bring your words to life," says Pasek. Writing musicals for Broadway is no easy feat, but Pasek and Paul have some advice for young story-tellers: "Let your imagination run wild. Keep asking the question '**WHAT IF?**' What if a character did this? What if a character did that? Be creative and allow your mind to think of the range of possibilities a story could go, and then write it!"

If you CHOSE ⬇ THAT:

While some artists use clay or bronze to make sculptures, if you follow in the footsteps of Nathan Sawaya you'll use—**LEGOS!** Sawaya was a lawyer in New York City before he quit his job to become a Lego sculptor. He developed his lifelong passion for the toys and has since become an internationally famous artist. Sawaya's artworks are painstakingly constructed out of **THOUSANDS OF BRICKS**, and sometimes it takes him months to finish just one sculpture! He sketches out his ideas before beginning a project, and then he dives into the more than 2.5 million bricks he has in his New York and Los Angeles art studios. Sawaya says, "A life-size human form sculpture typically has 15,000 [to] 25,000 bricks."

a creation by Nathan Sawaya made of Lego bricks

CHOOSE THIS:

Everyone knows your face.

CHOOSE THAT:

You like being in disguise.

MUSE BEFORE YOU CHOOSE

People say hi to you wherever you go. No privacy. Stay anonymous. Scratchy wigs and fake mustaches.

If you CHOSE THIS:

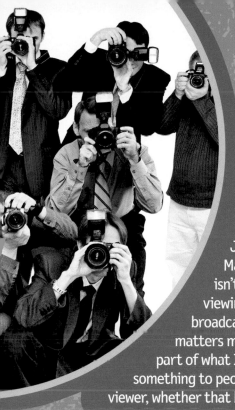

You may like being **RECOGNIZED** by people, but when you're a **NEWS ANCHOR,** the audience doesn't necessarily tune in to see your **PRETTY FACE**—they watch to get the scoop on world events. Jackie Ward of Channel 6 News in Portland, Maine, U.S.A., says, "As a reporter, the story isn't about me. It's about the person I'm interviewing or the topic I'm covering." A career in broadcast journalism involves getting to know what matters most in people's lives. Ward says, "My favorite part of what I do is being able to tell stories that mean something to people. My goal is to draw **EMOTION** out of the viewer, whether that be joy, anger, sorrow, or inspiration."

If you CHOSE THAT:

Being a **SPY** in disguise for the CIA—the Central Intelligence Agency—may sound fun and cool, but there's a whole lot more to the job than fake mustaches. The agency is responsible for providing **INFORMATION** to the U.S. government that protects **NATIONAL INTERESTS** and **SECURITY.** Working in the Directorate of Operations—the spying division—is only a small part of the agency and requires you to be on top of your game in every way. The CIA wants only the smartest candidates with strong analytical abilities, who also desire **TO SERVE** their country. You should learn a foreign language and keep a clean record. They'll look into your background with a fine-tooth comb!

CHOOSE

THIS:

Paint pictures with words.

or

CHOOSE

THAT:

Bring stories to life with pictures.

MUSE BEFORE YOU CHOOSE Gruesome grammar. Vivid verbs. Cleaning paintbrushes. Critics.

If you CHOSE THIS: ⬇

Ever consider writing a novel? What if you became as famous as Rick Riordan, author of the Percy Jackson series? Writing books isn't easy, but there are some things every aspiring novelist can do to improve his or her work. On his website, Riordan provides some helpful advice:

1. **FIND A TEACHER YOU RESPECT.** It's helpful if a young writer can find a mentor who believes in his or her talent. Don't be afraid to ask for help!

2. **READ A LOT!** You will learn the craft of writing by immersing yourself in the voices, styles, and structures of writers who have gone before you.

3. **WRITE EVERY DAY!** Keep a journal. Writing is like a sport—you only get better if you practice.

If you CHOSE THAT: ⬇

Maybe you should try becoming a children's book **ILLUSTRATOR!** Jerry Pinkney, the Caldecott Medal–winning illustrator of *The Lion & the Mouse,* says his favorite part of the job is the **CREATIVE PROCESS** behind bringing stories to life. "I love the act of making marks on paper, and seeing those marks develop into a picture. My intent and hope is to lead the viewer into a world that only exists because of that picture." As a kid, Pinkney suffered from **DYSLEXIA**—a reading disorder—but he never let it stop him from doing well in school and becoming one of America's most beloved illustrators. Pinkney says, "For the young person who is struggling in school, never forget there are many **DIFFERENT WAYS TO LEARN.** Do not be afraid to try. Do not be disappointed when making mistakes. Everything that happens to you will frame who you are, and who you will become. Your path to success will follow."

ANALYZE THIS!

If you mostly picked **CHOOSE THIS,** you are a creator who loves the spotlight! Your personality is ideal for high-profile jobs that bring lots of public attention. Whether you're involved in the arts, journalism, or dog-food tasting, you will enjoy knowing that the public gets to see and admire your work. This can be incredibly rewarding when things go well and the public adores you. However, life can quickly feel overwhelming when the reviews of your work are less than positive. Try to have thick skin and surround yourself with supportive people, and you'll be prepared for any outcome.

ANALYZE THAT!

If you mostly picked **CHOOSE THAT,** you love to dive in and get your hands dirty. You've got the brains to analyze your surroundings, but you'd rather jump in on the action! You probably have lightning-fast reflexes and a way out of any situation, and you're just the person to tackle tough jobs. But still, be careful not to rush into everything without thinking—you could end up in some sticky situations!

CHAPTER ⑧
The
SOCIAL
NETWORK

We humans are social creatures. That means we (generally) like groups, getting along with others, and having a network of friends to be there for us when we need to keep a chin up. But not all interactions are positive—life is full of frustrating moments when you just want to grit your teeth. This chapter is about some of the unique social situations we find ourselves in, so tread lightly as you enter the land of family, friends, and frenemies!

CHOOSE **THIS:**

Your friends are referred to as a **troop.**

or

CHOOSE **THAT:**

Your **family** can be such an **embarrassment.**

MUSE BEFORE YOU CHOOSE   Scouts and soldiers are also called troops. Awkward moments. Blushing.

138

If you CHOSE THIS: ⬇

You're **NOT NECESSARILY** in the Boy Scouts or Girl Scouts if you and your friends are called a troop. You could be a **KANGAROO!** A group of kangaroos can be called a troop and can range anywhere from a few individuals to more than a hundred. Known as a very social species, kangaroos engage in **"NOSE TOUCHING"** as a way of getting along, and males perform **BOXING** matches to show everybody who's boss. So you and your buddies will likely have a new routine of sniff-sniff, punch-punch when you say hello!

kangaroos

If you CHOSE THAT: ⬇

You must be a **PANDA**, because a group of the cuddly black-and-white bears is sometimes called an embarrassment. Pandas are not very social creatures, preferring to spend their days munching on **BAMBOO** in peace and quiet, but occasionally they'll gather for mating season in the spring. A female will deliver her cubs up to 160 days later and will raise them on her own. It's a pretty solitary life being a panda, and being called an **EMBARRASSMENT** must be pretty rough, too!

Think Twice!

A group of wombats is called a wisdom.

giant pandas

CHOOSE

THIS:

Go with the crowd.

African lions

or

CHOOSE

THAT:

Go solo.

MUSE BEFORE YOU CHOOSE

Following orders. Getting along with others. Be your own boss. Loneliness.

If you CHOSE ↓THIS:

You may find that being a member of a group has its advantages. Take **LIONS,** for example. Lions live in a pride with usually about **15 MEMBERS,** which allows them to hunt and defend themselves collectively. Lion prides oftentimes will attack one another to defend their territory, and having strength in numbers could mean the difference between **LIFE** and **DEATH.** So take comfort in your choice to hang with a **CROWD,** because at least you'll know you won't have to fight your battles alone!

If you CHOSE THAT: ↓

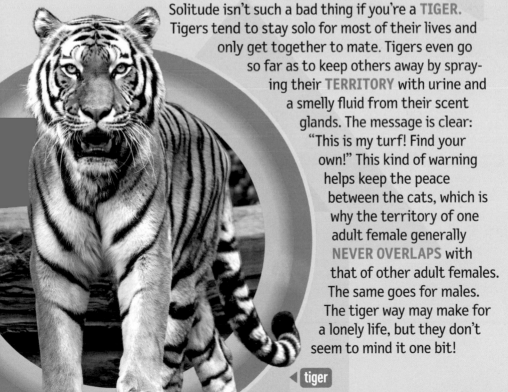

Solitude isn't such a bad thing if you're a **TIGER.** Tigers tend to stay solo for most of their lives and only get together to mate. Tigers even go so far as to keep others away by spraying their **TERRITORY** with urine and a smelly fluid from their scent glands. The message is clear: "This is my turf! Find your own!" This kind of warning helps keep the peace between the cats, which is why the territory of one adult female generally **NEVER OVERLAPS** with that of other adult females. The same goes for males. The tiger way may make for a lonely life, but they don't seem to mind it one bit!

◄ tiger

CHOOSE **THIS:**

Be the **star** athlete at your **school.**

or

CHOOSE **THAT:**

Be the smartest **kid** in your **school.**

MUSE BEFORE YOU CHOOSE

Sports scholarships. Going pro. Straight A's. Going to the best college.

If you CHOSE ↓THIS:

Turns out that being a good athlete has a lot to do with your attitude, not just your innate talents. Dr. Patrick Cohn specializes in **SPORTS PSYCHOLOGY** strategies, and he says that your mind—what you think and believe—is your best asset in becoming a better player. "Most young athletes lack **CONFIDENCE** for three common reasons: 1) They don't know **HOW TO IMPROVE**, other than with more practice; 2) Their **BELIEF IN THEMSELVES** changes from play to play; and 3) They had difficult **PAST FAILURES**. I help my athletes understand these negative beliefs so they can start the next game or match with a higher level of confidence."

If you CHOSE THAT:↓

Making yourself **SMARTER** is definitely a possibility, according to recent psychological studies. Researchers say intelligence is changeable—not fixed—meaning that if you weren't born a genius there's still hope for you to improve your smarts. **HAVING CONFIDENCE** has been proven to significantly raise the test scores of seventh graders, regardless of race or gender. But just believing "you can do it" doesn't get you to be the smartest kid in school. You still have to **WORK REALLY HARD**, do your homework, and turn it in on time. But at least you know it's within reach!

CHOOSE THIS:

Stay connected with your friends at all times.

CHOOSE THAT:

Keep some private moments to yourself.

MUSE BEFORE YOU CHOOSE

Stay up to speed. Everybody knows your business. Peace and quiet. You might miss out on something.

IF YOU CHOSE THIS:

You might suffer from "**FOMO**," or the fear of missing out! FOMO is anxiety about not being a part of a social event. That could include birthday parties, meeting up after school to hang out, or even just being in a group text—pretty much anything you *could* be doing that you're not *actually* doing. People with FOMO usually are big **SOCIAL NETWORKERS** and spend a lot of time keeping track of their friends and acquaintances on Facebook, Instagram, and other sites. The downside to FOMO is that if you're constantly looking to be included someplace else, you're not giving **QUALITY** to whatever it is you're doing instead. So if you find yourself left out, try cutting yourself some slack!

IF YOU CHOSE THAT:

It sounds like you may be practicing the art of "**JOMO**," or the joy of missing out. Coined by tech blogger Anil Dash, it's the exact opposite of FOMO (above). JOMO describes the act of giving yourself **SPACE** to think and experience things without anxiety about what you "should" be doing instead. Allowing ourselves some peaceful moments can be a challenge, especially in this high-tech age, but scientists say it's worth it. Reducing **SOCIAL STRESSES** is good for the heart and soul, so to speak.

CHOOSE

THIS:

You're **terrified** of making **decisions.**

or

CHOOSE

THAT:

You're afraid of being looked at.

 MUSE BEFORE YOU CHOOSE

Constant uncertainty. Takes a long time to order at restaurants. Wearing masks. School presentations are the worst.

If you CHOSE ⬇THIS:

If you're afraid of making decisions, then this book must be TORTURE for you! DECIDOPHOBIA, a condition coined by a university professor in the 1970s, is the fear of MAKING THE WRONG CHOICE. This causes you to not make a decision at all! Life is full of options, and the choices we make help determine who we are and who we will become. In a way it's kind of exciting to think we are in charge of our own destinies—it's like having a SUPERPOWER propelling us into the future. So don't fret too much about making the wrong choice—it can be a lot of fun! This book is good practice!

If you CHOSE ⬇THAT

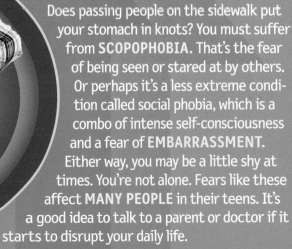

Does passing people on the sidewalk put your stomach in knots? You must suffer from SCOPOPHOBIA. That's the fear of being seen or stared at by others. Or perhaps it's a less extreme condition called social phobia, which is a combo of intense self-consciousness and a fear of EMBARRASSMENT. Either way, you may be a little shy at times. You're not alone. Fears like these affect MANY PEOPLE in their teens. It's a good idea to talk to a parent or doctor if it starts to disrupt your daily life.

THAT:
Big bear hugs!

or

THIS:
Long-distance kisses!

MUSE BEFORE YOU CHOOSE Grumpy grizzlies. Cuddly embraces. Not as personal. You won't get the flu.

If you CHOSE ⬇THIS:

Everybody needs a hug to lift our spirits from time to time. It turns out that a **HUG** can also be good for your **HEART**, especially if you're squeezing a robot named **HUGBOT**. After a five-second embrace, sensors in HugBot will read your pulse and provide medical information about your **BLOOD PUMPER**. The designers hope HugBot will be installed in schools and children's hospitals to share some love and keep people informed about their health.

If you CHOSE THAT:⬇

Pucker up! Smooching from a distance has been made possible by **KISSENGER**, a robot that allows you to transmit **DIGITAL KISSES** to a loved one far away. The egg-shaped machine is equipped with sensors that can distinguish the shape of the kisser's mouth and the varying degrees of **PRESSURE** in the lips. Your loved one holds Kissenger up to his or her lips or cheek and receives your kiss in real time!

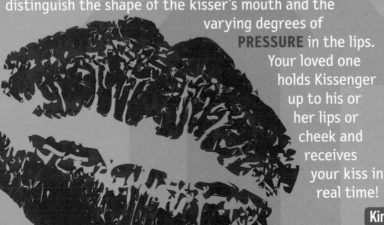

Think Twice!

In 2013, Japan launched a cute robot named Kirobo into space to serve as a friendly companion for astronauts.

Kirobo ▶

CHOOSE THIS:

You are a warrior.

army ants

MUSE
BEFORE YOU
CHOOSE

Battle scars. Keeping your guard up. Heavy lifting. Design your dream home!

or

CHOOSE THAT:

You are a builder.

termite mound

If you CHOSE

THIS:

You might not think humans and **ANTS** have much in common—but you'd be WRONG! Humans and ants both amass armies and wage war on their own kind, which is pretty unique in the animal kingdom. Other animals—like chimpanzees and killer whales—have been known to get into **ORGANIZED** battles, but by "war" we're talking **LARGE-SCALE ATTACKS**, involving thousands of soldiers. War also involves strategy, and ants are known for making good decisions collectively when faced with tough choices. That's why a group of ants is called an **ARMY!**

Choice Nugget

The aardvark is one of the termite's worst enemies. It claws through the termite mound and uses its long, sticky tongue to gobble up the insects inside.

If you CHOSE THAT:

Do you feel unique? Humans are the only mammal to have complex societies that can also build structures to contain them. The **TERMITE** is the closest animal that achieves such architectural wonders. Colonies of the Formosan subterranean termite have been known to build mounds up to **50 FEET** (15 m) tall. They are famous for their unique system of passageways that allow air to circulate, cooling the entire structure and maintaining a temperature of about 90°F (32°C). These impressive mounds are made with piles of termite **DUNG**, which might make you wonder what a skyscraper of human poop would look (and smell) like!

151

LET'S SEE WHAT **YOUR CHOICES** SAY **ABOUT YOU.**

DOC TALK ...

PSYCHOLOGIST
DR. MATT BELLACE
DISSECTS YOUR
DECISIONS ...

ANALYZE THIS!

If you mostly picked **CHOOSE THIS,** you're an outgoing, extroverted person who deeply values a connection with others. The good news is that surrounding yourself with positive social support could help you live a longer and happier life. However, maintaining high levels of popularity can be exhausting. You may find that responding to constant text messages and invites becomes increasingly difficult, and that making simple decisions can be tough when you care a lot about other people's opinions. The bottom line is, enjoy everything in moderation—even your social life!

ANALYZE THAT!

If you mostly picked **CHOOSE THAT,** you're a quiet, introverted person who values time to yourself. Let's face it, interacting with people can be draining. Plus, you know that you can probably get more done on your own. Taking quality alone time can be a great way to destress and to get to know yourself. The downside of having so much alone time is that it can be very, well ... lonely. Introverts like you may not need as much social interaction as most people, but your friends and family are still important. Even if it's in small doses, make time to connect with others.

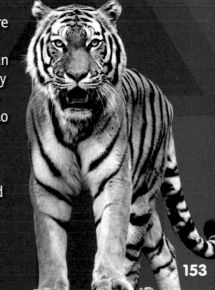

CHAPTER 9

TRICK or TREAT

No, this chapter isn't about Halloween, so take off your costume. This is a game—a deliciously evil game—where your decisions will either make or break you. One choice will lead you to something you might want, while the other ... well, let's just say you might need to review your answers to the survival questions in Chapter 2. Will you end up relaxing on vacation? Or will you end up wishing you had stayed home instead? Do your best to choose wisely—but don't be surprised if you encounter some less-than-desirable outcomes. Bwahahaha!

THIS:

Spend an **hour** in a **cave** without a **flashlight.**

or

luminescent bugs in a cave in Waitomo, New Zealand

THAT:

Spend a **month** at the **beach** on an Australian **island.**

Christmas Island red crabs

MUSE
BEFORE YOU
CHOOSE

Bats ... lots of bats. Creepy crawlies. Relaxing by the sea. Sand in your pants.

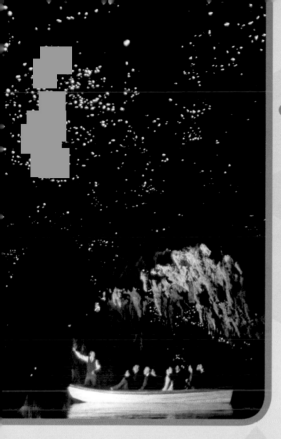

If you CHOSE ←THIS:

You're in for a TREAT. Even without a flashlight, the caves of **WAITOMO** in New Zealand are full of light, thanks to the glowworm *Arachnocampa luminosa*. The **LUMINESCENT BUGS** spin sticky silk threads that hang from the cave ceiling to ensnare their prey, which is mostly flies, mosquitoes, and moths. They live here because they must be in a place with very little wind, so their threads don't get tangled and stuck together. Their **GLOWING** quality creates an effect similar to a **STARRY NIGHT SKY** and can be quite breath-taking to behold. Enjoy the show!

If you CHOSE THAT:

You've been TRICKED. Good luck trying to catch some rays on the beaches of **CHRISTMAS ISLAND** near Indonesia. You're in for a crabby surprise! Sometime between October and December (depending on weather conditions), an estimated 120 million **RED CRABS** (*Gecarcoidea natalis*) migrate several miles from their cushy burrows in the island's interior to the sandy shores. Watch where you step so you don't get pinched, because these crabs are on a mission to get to the ocean and mate. Once their **MISSION** is accomplished, the crabs make their way back to their **BURROWS,** where they spend most of the year.

It Gets Worse!

While you're on Christmas Island, be on the lookout for swarms of *Anoplolepis gracilipes*, also called yellow crazy ants (yes, that's their real name). The ants are known for their wild movements when disturbed.

CHOOSE **THIS:**

Smell a **flower.**

or

CHOOSE **THAT:**

Smell a **toilet** bowl.

**MUSE
BEFORE YOU
CHOOSE**

Delightful fragrance. Allergies. Explosive diarrhea—need we say more?

If you CHOSE THIS: ⬇

You've been TRICKED. Your nostrils aren't prepared for the stinking **CORPSE FLOWER** (*Amorphophallus titanum*), a rare type of lily from the rain forests of Sumatra. It emits a **SMELL** similar to **ROTTING FLESH** to attract pollinators like flies and carrion beetles, which normally go after dead animals. Also the world's **LARGEST FLOWER**, with some blooms reaching almost 12 feet (3.5 m) tall, the corpse plant can spend more than **A DECADE** between blooms. Huge crowds of plant enthusiasts gather at a blooming for a smell of its rare stench, so you won't be alone when you take a whiff.

corpse flower

If you CHOSE THAT: ⬇

You're in for a TREAT. Well, kind of. It *is* still a toilet, after all. The **SOLID GOLD TOILET** made by a jeweler in Hong Kong, China, is believed to be the most expensive bottom throne on the planet, valued at about **$5 MILLION.** The Hang Fung Gold Technology Group built the john in 2001, when gold was much cheaper than it is today. You probably won't mind the smell, because it's off-limits to tourists and is well taken care of. Good luck convincing the jeweler to let you **TAKE A SNIFF!**

solid gold toilet in Hong Kong, China

Think Twice!

The most expensive toilet ever built may be the one constructed for the International Space Station by NASA. Estimated to cost $19 million, it recycles urine into water.

CHOOSE

THIS:

Knife noises

or

CHOOSE

THAT:

Swamp sounds

MUSE BEFORE YOU CHOOSE

Loud cutlery. Blade melodies. Outdoor concert. Marshy music.

If you CHOSE ⬇ THIS:

You've been TRICKED. You'll want some earplugs, because a study found that the **SCREECH** of a knife scraping a glass bottle has been identified as the **WORST SOUND** to the human ear. Scientists who study the brain's response to unpleasant sounds found that noises with a frequency between **2,000 AND 5,000 HERTZ** were the hardest to bear. This range includes fingernails on a chalkboard and a fork scraping glass. These unpleasant sounds activate a region in the brain that processes **EMOTIONS**, which explains why we have such a strong reaction when we hear them.

If you CHOSE ⬇ THAT:

You're in for a TREAT. An online competition called "The **MOST BEAUTIFUL SOUND** in the World," has identified a swamp in Malaysia as having a particularly pleasant sound. Photographer Marc Anderson set up multidirectional microphones in Kubah National Park and recorded a variety of animals communicating before nightfall. Anderson describes the experience: "The forest was **PULSING WITH LIFE**—cicadas, frogs, birds, insects. I don't know if I've heard a richer natural chorus than that afternoon in Kubah." Who knew swamp things could sound so nice?

CHOOSE THIS:

royal jelly, a bee secretion

Smear baby food on your face.

or

CHOOSE THAT:

MUSE BEFORE YOU CHOOSE

Easy snack. Mushy vegetables on your nose. Warms you head to toe. Mysterious ingredients.

Slurp down a bowl of nutritious soup.

IF YOU CHOSE THIS:

You're in for a TREAT. No, you don't get to have a fun food fight with strained peas and carrots. This baby food is called **ROYAL JELLY**, and it's a secretion made by worker bees that is fed to **LARVAE**—bee babies—for a short time, but it is the only thing that the bee destined to be future queen of the hive eats. Considered to be one of the world's most **NUTRIENT-RICH** substances, royal jelly is used as an ingredient in many skin-care products to enhance the skin's texture. You may not need it now, but when you're older you might find yourself smearing on some bee baby food!

Choice Nugget

Want more stinky food? Try the durian. This fruit from southeast Asia has a smell that's been compared to roadkill.

IF YOU CHOSE THAT:

You've been TRICKED. If the smell of **WET SOCKS** sounds appetizing, then we've got the dish for you! Plug up your nose for a bowl of soup made with *cheonggukjang*, a **FERMENTED SOYBEAN PASTE** popular in Korean cuisine that's known for its **ULTRAPUNGENT** aroma. It may smell like a dead body, but this food is rich in vitamins and other nutrients believed to aid digestion. *Peee-yew!*

CHOOSE

THIS:

Discover gold and jewels.

or

CHOOSE

THAT:

Uncover forgotten temples.

MUSE BEFORE YOU CHOOSE   What would Indiana Jones do?

If you CHOSE ⬇ THIS:

elaborately decorated relic of St. Valerius

You've been TRICKED. If bling is your thing, you'll be surprised—and maybe grossed out—by these **JEWEL-ENCRUSTED SKELETONS.** Originally unearthed in the late 16th century in the catacombs of Rome, the skeletons were sent to churches in Germany, Switzerland, and Austria. The receiving churches then spent years adorning the **BONES** with **RARE JEWELS** and gold clothing, even filling the eye sockets, until it became unfashionable to spend so much money on such fineries. Not quite what you had in mind, eh?

If you CHOSE ⬇ THAT:

You're in for a TREAT. Looking for lost cities is a whole lot easier thanks to a new technology called **LiDAR**—which stands for Light Detection and Ranging. **LASER BEAMS** pulse a million times every four seconds from a helicopter or airplane, revealing human-made structures hidden under thick forests. LiDAR came in handy in 2012 when scientists discovered new temples in the ancient city of **ANGKOR** in Cambodia. This new information told archaeologists exactly where they needed to dig, so they wouldn't waste time searching through the forest. Must be nice to know you won't be digging in the dark!

Angkor Wat temple, Angkor, Cambodia

CHOOSE **THIS:**

You've got a **stench, and most** animals steer **clear** of **you.**

or

CHOOSE **THAT:**

You're cute and **cuddly,** and **animals** like **you.**

Body odor. No furry friends. Photogenic. Predator pals.

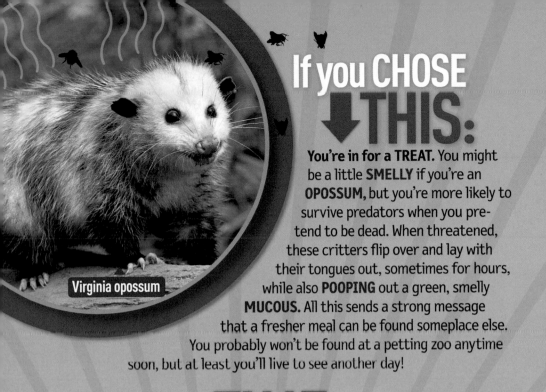

Virginia opossum

If you CHOSE ⬇ THIS:

You're in for a TREAT. You might be a little **SMELLY** if you're an **OPOSSUM,** but you're more likely to survive predators when you pretend to be dead. When threatened, these critters flip over and lay with their tongues out, sometimes for hours, while also **POOPING** out a green, smelly **MUCOUS.** All this sends a strong message that a fresher meal can be found someplace else. You probably won't be found at a petting zoo anytime soon, but at least you'll live to see another day!

If you CHOSE THAT: ⬇

You've been TRICKED. Being well liked in the animal kingdom isn't necessarily a good thing, especially if that means animals like to EAT you! Take the **CUTE AND CUDDLY CHIPMUNK.** Near the bottom of the food web, chipmunks are eaten by pretty much any animal quick enough to catch them. Hawks, snakes, foxes, and weasels love a chipmunk snack when they can get one. These cute animals may look adorable, but **DANGER** is always lurking around the corner!

chipmunk

Think Twice!

Fulmar chicks have the best of both worlds—they're both cute and cuddly while also equipped with a pretty gross defense mechanism. The baby birds projectile vomit a smelly, orange goo at the face of an approaching predator. The substance is so sticky that it glues the predator's feathers together.

CHOOSE THIS:

Hike through a forest that looks back at you.

or

CHOOSE THAT:

Walk through a building with walls that look back at you.

dolls on La Isla de las Muñecas, Mexico

MUSE BEFORE YOU CHOOSE

Nosy trees. Creepy camping. Spooky hallways. Sneaky spies.

If you CHOSE THIS:

You've been TRICKED. Perhaps one of the CREEPIEST places on the planet, La Isla de las Muñecas (ISLAND OF THE DOLLS) in Mexico is home to hundreds of abandoned dolls hanging from trees. According to legend, more than 50 years ago, Don Julian Santana moved onto the island in the middle of Teshuilo Lake. Some say a little girl drowned in the lake, while others think Don Julian only imagined the girl. We'll never know for sure, but what we do know is that he devoted his life to honoring this LOST SOUL by collecting dolls and suspending them from the trees, probably for her to play with in the AFTERLIFE. Be sure to take your pictures and get outta there. You wouldn't want to be stuck on the island after nightfall!

If you CHOSE THAT:

You're in for a TREAT. The walls of the GEORGIA AQUARIUM in Atlanta are full of eyes, but you won't mind what's looking back at you. More than 100,000 SEA CREATURES swim in more than 6 million gallons (22,704,000 L) of water, making this one of the world's largest aquariums. If you want a closer look, put on your wet suit and take a dive with the WHALE SHARKS on exhibit. They're the largest fish in the animal kingdom, but don't worry, they won't eat you—unless you're plankton!

Georgia Aquarium, Georgia, U.S.A.

CHOOSE

THIS:

Monster food

or

CHOOSE

THAT:

Dragon food

MUSE
BEFORE YOU
CHOOSE

Ghoulish grub. Messy. Flame-broiled. Too hot to handle.

If you CHOSE ⬇THIS:

You're in for a TREAT. An automotive company in the Czech Republic has created the world's biggest ice-cream **MONSTER TRUCK,** and there's a monster-size cone waiting for you! The 21-foot-tall (6.4 m) truck was made as a publicity stunt to promote the company throughout Europe. You'll need a **LADDER** to place your order, but the reward is some serious soft-serve!

If you CHOSE ⬇THAT:

You've been TRICKED. KOMODO DRAGONS are one of the world's **LEAST** picky eaters, which means they will devour just about anything—even YOU! The 330-pound (150 kg) lizard, which is found in Indonesia, will eat carrion (dead things), deer, pigs, smaller dragons, and even large water buffalo and humans. And it's not just their **RAZOR-SHARP** teeth you have to worry about—their saliva contains more than 50 strains of bacteria. Within 24 hours most bite victims suffer **BLOOD POISONING,** and guess who has been patiently waiting nearby? The dragon calmly hangs out near its victim until it's good and ready to be devoured!

Komodo dragon

LET'S SEE WHAT **YOUR CHOICES** SAY **ABOUT YOU.**

DOC TALK ...

PSYCHOLOGIST DR. MATT BELLACE DISSECTS YOUR DECISIONS ...

ANALYZE
THIS!

If you mostly picked **CHOOSE THIS,** then it's possible that you just might be a little gullible. It's okay to be trusting, but remember to do your research and think things through before making a snap decision. If it sounds too good to be true, it probably is!

ANALYZE
THAT!

If you mostly picked **CHOOSE THAT,** then congratulations, because you have the ability to read between the lines! You can sniff out when someone is saying something they don't mean, or vice versa. This can be really important in life, especially when dealing with shady characters! Just don't be too suspicious of everyone; after all, it's good to be able to trust the people who are close to you.

Credits

Published by the National Geographic Society
Gary E. Knell, *President and Chief Executive Officer*
John M. Fahey, *Chairman of the Board*
Declan Moore, *Executive Vice President; President, Publishing and Travel*
Melina Gerosa Bellows, *Publisher; Chief Creative Officer,
     Books, Kids, and Family*

Prepared by the Book Division
Hector Sierra, *Senior Vice President and General Manager*
Nancy Laties Feresten, *Senior Vice President, Kids Publishing and Media*
Jennifer Emmett, *Vice President, Editorial Director, Kids Books*
Eva Absher-Schantz, *Design Director, Kids Publishing and Media*
Jay Sumner, *Director of Photography, Kids Publishing*
R. Gary Colbert, *Production Director*
Jennifer A. Thornton, *Director of Managing Editorial*

Staff for This Book
Ariane Szu-Tu, *Project Manager*
Julide Dengel, *Art Director*
Simon Renwick, *Designer*
Hillary Leo, *Photo Editor*
Paige Towler, *Editorial Assistant*
Sanjida Rashid, *Design Production Assistant*
Margaret Leist, *Photo Assistant*
Grace Hill, *Associate Managing Editor*
Mike O'Connor, *Production Editor*
Lewis R. Bassford, *Production Manager*
Susan Borke, *Legal and Business Affairs*

Production Services
Phillip L. Schlosser, *Senior Vice President*
Chris Brown, *Vice President, NG Book Manufacturing*
George Bounelis, *Senior Production Manager*
Nicole Elliott, *Director of Production*
Rachel Faulise, *Manager*
Robert L. Barr, *Manager*